Take Stock

Revised Edition

A Roadmap to Profiting From Your
First Walk Down Wall Street

By

Ellis Traub

TAKE STOCK, REVISED EDITION
EDITED BY JODI BRANDON
TYPESET BY EILEEN DOW MUNSON
Cover design by Foster & Foster, Inc.
Printed in the U.S.A. by Book-mart Press

To order this title, please call toll-free 1-800-CAREER-1 (NJ and Canada: 201-848-0310) to order using VISA or MasterCard, or for further information on books from Career Press.

The Career Press, Inc., 3 Tice Road, PO Box 687,
Franklin Lakes, NJ 07417
www.careerpress.com

Library of Congress Cataloging-in-Publication Data

Traub, Ellis.
    Take stock! : a roadmap to profiting from your first walk down Wall Street / by
Ellis Traub.—Rev. ed.
        p. cm.
    Includes bibliographical references and index.
    ISBN 1-56414-800-9 (paper)
        1. Investments. 2. Stocks. 3. Portfolio management. I. Title.

HG4521.T683 2005
332.63'22--dc22

                                                                    2004058645

To Dianne,

who told me I could;

and to David,

who told me I should.

Acknowledgments

In addition to those close to me to whom this book is dedicated, many people had a part to play in making this book happen.

Certainly George Nicholson and Tom O'Hara deserve the credit for devising a simple and successful investment methodology and having the vision and selfless determination to build an organization to share with the rest of the world—the National Association of Investors Corporation (NAIC).

I want to express my deep gratitude to Phil Keating, constant friend and mentor, for introducing me to NAIC and shepherding me through my latter-day education.

My thanks also go to Don Danko, longtime editor-in-chief of *Better Investing* magazine, and his worthy colleague, Mark Robertson, both of whom have inspired and encouraged me to stay focused on the purity of the mission—to empower every man to invest successfully—as they have so faithfully.

And my wife, Dianne, who turned out to be not only my main supplier of moral support but a very capable and relentless resident editor as well, for which I must add my gratitude.

Contents

Why You Need This Book

Since November 2000, when the first edition of *Take Stock* was published, many events have occurred to make the investing climate tumultuous. The stock market bubble of that time finally burst as predicted, to be followed by as staggering a bust and, finally, a return to relative normalcy. Our nation was attacked on our own precious soil by a virulent and elusive foreign enemy. Our country's military has become engaged in a bitter and seemingly hopeless quagmire overseas. Our politicians have irresponsibly polarized and divided our nation as never before. And our economy has faked out the economists by first neglecting to follow typical cycles and then careening into a recession and recovery as if to make up for lost time.

All of this has taken its toll on investors, many of whom played the game and lost their nerve at just the wrong time. Sadly, a new legion of financially walking wounded has staggered away from the investment battlefield vowing to never again risk their money in common stocks.

Not long after the publication of the first edition of this book, I was flattered to be invited to take part in a competition sponsored by the American Association of Individual Investors (AAII). The contest was a regular feature that typically pitted three well-known professionals against each other, each investing a hypothetical $100,000 and managing that portfolio for a six-month period. I entered it reluctantly, protesting that a) I was not a professional, and b) the six-month period was not at all a reasonable period over which to measure success for a long-term investor. I agreed only when they assured me that I could use the opportunity afforded by the biweekly commentary to tout the virtues of long-term investing and to make it clear that I had no illusions about "winning" over the short term. Interestingly enough, we selected 14 stocks, retained them through the entire period (should have replaced one of them but didn't), and still beat the professionals—and the S&P 500—by more than 20 percent!

This was something of a fluke, of course. I could have just as easily lost in the short term. But I did pick excellent companies using the principles detailed in this book, whereas my professional colleagues frantically bought and sold in a counter-productive effort to catch up.

I don't mention this for the purpose of blowing my horn. As I said, it could have gone the other way. I mention this to make the point that one doesn't have to be a professional to be successful, and everything that's happened between the first publication and this one has only confirmed and reinforced the principles contained herein.

The stock market does flit hither and yon, buffeted by the perceptions of its participants. And those who chase those perceptions and trade in the short term are most likely to suffer. On the other hand, those who recognize the basic facts that good companies will always make a profit over the long haul and that investing involves owning pieces of those good companies will always profit from it and will make out no matter what goes on in the world.

This edition doesn't change any of the basics. They are timeless. It does seek to update those things that relate to the world today and to capitalize on the lessons learned from the events that have transpired in the intervening months.

What makes this book better than—or even different from—any other investment book? After all, there are thousands of them out there competing for your attention.

First of all, it's about something you've likely never heard of: *technamental investing*. Actually, the only thing new about this discipline is its name. Its roots are embedded in a methodology that's been practiced with enormous success by more than 5 million investors for nearly a half century. First taught by the original founders of the National Association of Investors Corporation (NAIC), George A. Nicholson Jr., Thomas E. O'Hara, Frederick C. Russell, and a few others, it's been spread across the nation—around the world, in fact—by a zealous corps of volunteers.

Technamental investing has been referred to at various times as "growth/ value," "long-term," "fundamental," "buy and hold," or simply "NAIC-type" investing; even NAIC has not put a name to it. But each of these terms describes a facet of technamental investing. I've coined that term because, in my opinion, it captures the essence of what we do. And what we do should have a name.

The investment community likes to make a sharp distinction between fundamental analysis and technical analysis, as well it should, because they are as far apart in practice as heaven and hell. Technical analysis involves graphing and visually analyzing the movement and volume of the overall market and the prices of its individual stocks. Over the years, scores of hopeful amateurs and erudite academics have sought—and have even named—repetitive price and volume patterns in an effort to find some consistent relationship between the historical movement of stock prices and their future movement. They've had little success. It seems to me that, if any of the hundreds of technical approaches—stochastics, momentum investing, moving averages, and so forth—were effective, there would be only that one!

Fundamental analysis is the study of the fundamentals of companies—their actual operation and financial condition. Without question, the changes in a company's fundamentals—its revenues, earnings, profit margins, and other data that address the lifeblood of a company—can have an enormous impact on the future performance of a stock. Patterns here can easily be seen, are not at all hard to interpret, and have a great deal of predictive value.

The "technical" component of technamental investing is the use of charts and visual analysis. It capitalizes on the belief that pictures are indeed worth thousands of words—and volumes of numbers. It puts the "fun" back into fundamental analysis, which seems to have become unnecessarily sophisticated and too mysterious for the average person.

My challenge is to cut the fundamentals down to size and make them simple enough for a grade-school kid or his grandma to understand. By explaining technamental analysis, which converts much of the mysterious stuff into pictures, hopefully I've met that challenge here.

The second reason this book is a must is that it is virtually the first book on the shelves that presents a demonstrably successful and elegantly simple investment discipline—*simply*.

The third reason is that investing—making money in the stock market—should be neither dangerous, tedious, nor time-consuming. It should be fun! This book should entertain you as you learn how to become financially successful.

NAIC, a nonprofit organization, was launched in 1951. Perhaps one of the better-kept national secrets, the association has always been a bit bashful about blowing its own horn. (I think it's time to do a little crowing on its behalf!)

Its wonderful volunteers, in more than 100 chapters across the country, put on thousands of events every year, all across the country. The sole purpose of those events is to convince people who are afraid of the stock market that they don't need to be—to empower people to make their own decisions about what stocks to buy and how long to hold on to them.

Small wonder that the financial press seems to pretend that this evangelical movement isn't there. It's understandable that publicity is rare concerning an organization whose approach and mission would deprive so many professionals of their fees.

Only when a maverick such as Peter Lynch comes along and devotes a chapter of a bestseller such as *Beating the Street* to extolling NAIC's virtues, or when the Beardstown Ladies make a splash, do the phones ring off the walls at NAIC's headquarters in Madison Heights, Michigan. Otherwise, it's hard to find the smallest mention in the regular press about the monthly events that NAIC chapters sponsor at a low cost or free of charge.

Though I give full credit to NAIC for introducing me to the philosophy behind technamental investing, I make no claim that the organization approves, endorses, or even agrees with my interpretation of its methods or with my approach. That said, NAIC *did* commission us ("us" being my company, Inve$tWare) to develop its official software and electronically implement its methods; so I suppose that might entitle us to some such credential. But I seek neither NAIC's approval nor its endorsement.

I am deeply grateful to NAIC for having made a huge difference in my life, and I am hopeful that this book will do all that is possible to stimulate public interest in that organization and to attract members and volunteers to its ranks.

Being a part of NAIC is the best way I know for you to learn the ropes and to follow up on what you will learn from this book. The organization offers countless resources to those who want to acquire wealth on their own.

I don't expect you to take anything on faith. NAIC members who have followed their organization's methods diligently have been able to pick four out of five winners and have been able to double their money every five years. This is an established fact and is part of NAIC lore.

However, I challenge you to weigh what you're about to read on the scales of logic and common sense. Ask yourself whether what you are reading makes sense to you. If it does, then look for the flaws. Only after you find that you can't poke holes in the logic should you put the principles to work for yourself and "put your money where *our* mouth is."

What you are about to read should both inspire and educate you. In Chapter 1, I'll tell you just why a college dropout such as me, with no education in finance, is the logical person to write this book.

Then, in Chapter 2, I'll go to work. I'll tell you that common stocks are the most lucrative investment you can make, and I'll explain why.

In Chapter 3, I'll convince you that you can do it, that technamental investing is not beyond you or over your head, and, in Chapter 4, I'll prove my point by introducing you to the only 10 terms you need to know.

In Chapter 5, I'll build on the terms you have learned and introduces you to the concept of growth, which is central to technamental investing.

In Chapter 6, I'll tell you where to find candidates for consideration and how to select them: what you should look for, what you should avoid. A number of changes have taken place since the first edition of *Take Stock*, especially with regard to the Internet and the availability of data.

In Chapters 7 and 8, I'll apply what you learned about growth to help you decide if a company is of good enough quality for you to consider buying its stock.

In Chapter 9, I'll deal with management's "report card," which enables you to assess management's ability to maintain a company's winning track record.

Assessing the quality of your prospective investment is the most important task; however, a good stock at a price that is too high is not a good investment. In Chapter 10, I'll lead you through the steps required to analyze the potential reward of buying a particular stock, to assess the risk involved, and to determine what a fair price would be.

In Chapter 11, I'll tell you how to compare companies in which you're interested in to find out which would be the best stock to add to your portfolio.

In Chapter 12, I'll cover portfolio management. With these easily employed defensive and offensive technamental strategies, you can ensure that your entire portfolio doesn't suffer from the misfortunes that can befall any specific stock you own, and you can achieve the highest return possible.

Finally, in Chapter 13, I'll deal with the things that I left out of the basic explanation because they aren't necessary and can be confusing or misleading. The chapter includes some of the strategies that you might later use to fine-tune your investing process, and it does so with the warning that you should use them with great care.

Appendix A in this edition is titled "The Stuff You Don't Need to Know" and fills a gap that some have mentioned when they critiqued the first.

Finally, Appendix B introduces you to the computer software that is available to implement this methodology. The number of software products to implement this methodology has grown since the last edition of this book, and I've made an effort to include all I consider worthy with a brief description of each.

When the first edition of *Take Stock* was published, many readers had a computer of their own or had one available, but many did not. Nowadays, most of you who read this book have—or have access to—a computer. Although the methods described in this book are just as valid for people who are equipped with only a pencil, a ruler, and a financial calculator, in this edition I have omitted the detailed instructions for doing stock studies manually. (Those who may still have such an interest may obtain those detailed instructions by writing to me at *etraub@financialliteracy.us*.

If you have access to a computer, I would strongly urge you to take a few moments before you get started and install the CD you'll find at the end of this book. It contains quizzes to reinforce what you learn from each chapter. It has a section on "Dealing with Data" that helps to solidify what you learn about the things you need to know about a company in Chapter 4. And it provides you with an automated worksheet that you can use right along with the text beginning in Chapter 10 and that you can use afterward to study any company you would like to do on your own. It also gives you older data for about 30 or so companies you can practice with.

I hope that this introduction to technamental investing will be an enjoyable and profitable adventure for you, and I wish you well on your journey.

CHAPTER 1

Look Who's Talking!

F irst, let me tell you why I think I'm qualified to write this book and why I'm presumptuous enough to offer you advice about investing.

Right off the bat, I'll tell you what I'm not. I am not an MBA, a CFA, or a CFP. My letterhead doesn't include a wake of alphabet soup trailing after my name. I'm not a professional money manager, a securities analyst, a college professor, or a stockbroker. In fact, I don't even have a degree! I did attend college, but I dropped out of Harvard when the Korean War broke out in 1951.

Determined to postpone my education until I could figure out what I really wanted to do for a living, I applied for both the Air Force and the Navy pilot training programs and opted to train with the Navy. Later, I took my commission in the U.S. Marine Corps, with which I served in the Korean theater as an all-weather fighter pilot. Fortunately for me, the war ended before I saw any serious action.

I returned to school in 1956, this time to Cornell University, where I studied hotel administration. Again my interests changed and, although I was on the dean's list, I left to fly for Eastern Airlines, embarking on a career that spanned the next 31 years. I also became a spokesman for the Air Line Pilots Association (ALPA) and handled public relations for that organization in South Florida for 14 years.

Frustrated by the responses that I received from management when I tried to suggest ideas to improve the company's operations, I started a movement to infuse participative management into Eastern's corporate culture. When Frank Borman, then Eastern's chairman and CEO, later made the effort to effect such a cultural change, I worked actively with Eastern's consultants, picking up yet another set of skills.

Eventually disheartened by the continuing impasse between labor and management, and dismayed at the direction that my cherished profession had taken, I retired from Eastern in 1988, three years before my age would have forced me to. Armed with glowing testimonials from both Borman and his adversary, Charles Bryan, the head of the combative machinists' union, I hung out my shingle as a management consultant in labor relations, community relations, and conflict management.

It was at that point that I again made a midcourse correction in my eclectic career and discovered the investment philosophy that changed my life forever.

My past investing experience had been nothing short of a disaster. Years earlier, in 1972, with four sons nearing college age, I had realized that my savings were inadequate to finance their education. I had neither put aside enough money to provide for it, nor properly managed the money I had saved.

Nineteen seventy-two was an election year, and I had become actively interested in the presidential campaign. One of the campaign workers I met was a stockbroker for a major firm. Thinking that he might be able to help with my financial predicament, I asked my new friend for some guidance.

His advice was this: "Because it's an election year, you should invest your savings in a hot stock and hold it until about two weeks before the election. The incumbents will do everything in their power to keep the economy strong as long as possible, so you can't go wrong. Sell your stock just before the election, and you'll be in clover!"

I not only invested all of my savings in a rapidly rising stock, but I borrowed on those holdings to buy more, and then borrowed more money on my signature to put into my prize investment. What did I know! Of course I had gambled and I lost. When shortly before the election I finally sold my holdings, I, along with half of Wall Street, found that I had taken a bath. All I had left was my considerable debt, my house, and, fortunately, a good job. Worst of all, the experience scared me out of the stock market for the next 15 years.

Fortunately, I didn't have access to my retirement fund in 1972, or I might have lost all of that as well. When I left Eastern many years later, most of my pension was intact, and I elected to accept it as a lump sum. Once again, I ventured into the stock market. This time, I was intent on *learning* what I needed to know to be successful. So I formed a committee consisting of two other people and myself. One member was another young, but far more knowledgeable and ethical, stockbroker. The second was my accountant.

The modus operandi was to be that we would make no decision unless it was unanimous. I believed that I could learn something from discussions involving the pros. As it worked out in practice, however, I would receive a call from Bill (the accountant) saying that he thought I should buy a certain stock. I would then call John (the broker) and ask what he thought. John would say, "Sounds like a good idea to me!" So I would buy the stock. Not much of an education there!

After about a year and a half of this process, and with all of my money invested, I sat at my computer to assess my progress and plot the trend. Sadly I discovered that if I continued to invest as I had been, in about nine years I'd be living under a bridge!

This happened on a Saturday. On the following day, serendipitously, an article appeared in the paper, written by Jim Russell, then the financial editor for the *Miami Herald.* At the end of the article Russell mentioned that on the following Saturday the National Association of Investors Corporation (NAIC) would be offering a seminar on how to evaluate common stocks. (NAIC is a nonprofit membership organization whose goal is to empower both investment club members and individual investors to invest successfully in common stocks.)

That next Saturday my life radically changed. I spent four hours listening to Phil Keating, an investment professional and one of the 3,000-plus volunteers across the country who unselfishly donate their time to NAIC, talk about the organization's methodology. Amazed at the method's elegant simplicity and at the cross section of people who attended and learned (there were no rocket scientists there), I sat entranced.

When I returned home that afternoon, I sat at my computer and entered all of the formulas and calculations I had just learned into a spreadsheet. By that night I was able to duplicate the tasks required to analyze a stock for prospective purchase.

From then on I was hooked. I attended workshops, learned the methodology well enough to teach it, and then volunteered to instruct others. My computer spreadsheet became more and more elaborate until it grew into a program called Take $tock, which embraced the NAIC methodology and included a few embellishments of my own. Not long thereafter I was invited to join NAIC's national computer organization, and NAIC asked me to let the organization market my software to its members.

Take $tock was so successful that NAIC invited me to develop its own official software product, and the Investor's Toolkit was born. Today about 50,000 investors use the toolkit, and each day another 20 to 30 join their ranks.

I continue to serve NAIC, now about a 200,000-member organization, as a volunteer and as a frequent speaker at its events across the country. In 1999, I was privileged to be the closing speaker at both of NAIC's national conventions.

Whereas once I was concerned about how long I might live before my funds ran out, now I could live forever—at least in terms of financial security. And today I chalk it all up to what I learned from NAIC.

Since the last edition of *Take Stock*, Inve$tWare Corporation, the company I founded and which served NAIC for so long, has merged with another company, ICLUBcentral of Cambridge, Massachusetts, and that company now provides all of the stock analysis software and club accounting software used by NAIC's members.

I have written this book hoping that the hundreds of thousands of others who know no more than I did back in 1972 might learn how to "Take $tock" and be successful investors without having to experience the angst that I did.

So that's who I am and why you have this book in your hands. Education, after all, is nothing more than a jump-start on experience. It allows us to learn from others' experiences so that we don't have to start from scratch. I hope that what I've written here will serve that purpose for you.

Let's Take Stock of the Mistakes I Made

Remember the kids' puzzle in the Sunday comics: "How many errors can you spot in this picture?" Here are my most significant mistakes, from which you can learn as I did:

➤ Not starting at an early age to put aside "untouchable" money for the future.

➤ Not properly investing the money I did put aside.

➤ Looking for advice from an unqualified person.

➤ Taking that advice.

➤ Investing all of my savings in a single "hot" stock.

➤ Borrowing on those holdings.

➤ Gambling with my remaining credit.

➤ Selling because of the price of the stock rather than the performance of the company.

➤ Staying away from the stock market after my disastrous first experience.

Unfortunately, these are the kinds of mistakes that we don't know are mistakes until it's too late and we suffer for them. Hopefully this book will help you to avoid the same mistakes before you, too, have to suffer. Better yet, perhaps this book will help you to accumulate wealth and become financially secure by taking the right steps before it's too late.

At this point, if you have a computer at your disposal, I would urge you to install the CD you'll find in the back of this book and take the first short quiz. You will find quizzes for each of the chapters to help reinforce what you've learned.

CHAPTER 2

Why Take Stock?

There are gazillions of investments to put your money into, so why should you be interested in stocks? If my assumption is correct—that you're interested in making money with your money and not simply indulging your ego with ownership, be it a painting or a professional ball team—then owning stocks is where it's at.

There are few things in which you can invest that are alive. Diamonds, though they sparkle, are dead. Paintings, whether of still lifes or live models, are said to have life if they're well done, but they lie dormant as they increase in value. Most of these "dead" objects increase in price because the dollars that were initially paid for them are the equivalent of more dollars today. In other words, inflation drives up the prices of inanimate objects. In addition to inflation, the relative scarcity of the kind of item you're holding will increase the perception of its value, so the price will increase as the item's perceived value increases. Sad but true, the value of a painting rises nicely when the artist dies.

Even bonds or Treasury bills that pay a fixed amount of interest are reasonably stable in price, except when interest rates fluctuate and the bonds are sold or purchased at more of less than their original price. Again, interest-rate changes, as with inflation, do not add real value to an investment.

What Is Money and How Is it Made?

To fully understand the significance of investing in something "live," which is central to technamental investing, let's take a quick run through something that you probably know but haven't thought much about. In order to build my case, I'm going to start at a point where everyone is in agreement—as rudimentary as it may be. So here goes.

Meet Oog and Mog. Oog was a fellow who lived in a cave when that lifestyle was the equivalent of living in our modern-day suburbia. Now Oog wasn't the hunter that Mog was. In fact, he couldn't run as fast or jump as high as Mog. If the truth were known, Oog was scared to death of saber-toothed tigers. But he had a special skill. He could make a heck of an arrowhead out of stone. And he learned to wrap it tightly on a pole, creating a mean spear.

Mog, on the other hand, was all thumbs when it came to tapping stones. He couldn't wrap the thongs around the poles; he simply didn't have the patience for it. But he was as brave as he was clumsy, and he was a heck of a hunter.

You already see where I'm going with this. Oog would make the spears for Mog, and Mog would give him meat in return. And this was how the concept of money began: with barter. One person would do something of value for another person, who would give back something of value to the first person.

Years later, Oog's and Mog's descendants began to exchange stones or animals' teeth for those goods or services. These tokens made barter more convenient. Tokens evolved into coins (introduced by the Lydians in the 17th century B.C.), and later into currency, or money (first introduced in China and many centuries later in late 18th-century France). As civilization progressed and goods and services proliferated beyond the point where people could meet at a marketplace and conduct their barter, money made it possible for each person to do what he or she did best when it was most convenient to do it. People could store up credits and use them for goods or services when the time was right.

The concept of currency has taken a beating in recent years as governments have postponed immediate trouble by printing more of it, by borrowing against future confiscation through taxation, and by otherwise cheapening its real value.

Still, nothing has really changed since Oog's time. The real value of money, and the way it is made, is timeless. To make money—to really create money and not just pass it around or diminish its value—one has to do one of two things: add value to a resource or provide a service that contributes to that effort.

Adding Value

Charlie, a construction worker, goes to work one morning and is told to dig a hole that measures 4 feet deep by 4 feet wide by 4 feet long. He finishes the task by noon.

When he comes back from lunch, his boss tells him that he's sorry, but the morning's work was a mistake. His job for the afternoon is to go get the dirt and sod and to make the hole he has just spent the morning digging disappear.

At the end of the day, when the afternoon's task has been completed, will Charlie have made any money? Charlie will *earn* money—he certainly deserves to be paid for his sweat and strain—but he will not have *made* anything! The wage paid to him for his effort will be a loss because that effort will add no value to any resource, nor will it provide a service of any value to anyone—not even his boss or his company.

What *is* worth the money is the value of what is *produced*, not the value of the input it took to produce it. (Wouldn't labor relations take a different direction if all parties thoroughly understood *that* concept!)

Providing a Service

Again, the key to the creation of wealth is adding value to a resource, or providing a valuable service and accumulating the rewards for doing so. Making steel out of ore, machining a part out of steel, building an automobile out of parts, and selling that automobile to the public—all are examples of adding value or providing a service. Manufacturing, information services, transportation, construction—whatever business you are in—must add value or provide a service that entices or induces someone who benefits from that value or service to pay for it.

It's rarely possible to add actual value to collectible objects or to income instruments such as corporate or government bonds. For that reason collectibles and bonds don't have nearly the investment potential that you'll find in a business.

Starting a Business

A business, on the other hand, is created for the sole purpose of adding value or performing services of value. Therefore, being in business is the key to the creation of wealth.

An entrepreneur dreams up an idea for something that she thinks will be of value, then follows through on it. Whether she's providing a product or a service, the enterprise involves substantial risk. No one can accurately predict how much demand there will be until the product or service is available, and no one can predict the cost of making it available until that cost has been paid. Nor can anyone predict whether demand for the product or service will last long enough for the entrepreneur to recover her investment.

Taking an idea from its birth in the brain to its tangible realization takes guts, intimacy with the product or service, and usually a whole lot of capital. Unfortunately, according to studies made for the U.S. Department of Commerce, more new companies go belly-up than survive.

That's why those who provide venture capital and start-up money to a new business demand and receive a sizeable chunk of the business and a substantial portion of the reward. And that's why you don't want to put your life's savings into someone else's new business. Even if the reward for picking a winner is fantastic, the chance of picking that winner is slim indeed. So leave the financing of new companies to those who know that business, who deal regularly with the odds, and who can afford the risks.

How about buying a business that's already successful? Maybe that's the ticket. Most of the initial risk is gone and the concept has already been proven. Instead of being 80-percent against you, the odds are somewhat more favorable.

Of course, the cost of buying such a business, now that the initial concerns have been laid to rest, would be much greater, because someone has already assumed the greater part of the risk and has done all of the start-up work.

Let's assume for the moment, however, that you have enough money to buy a business outright. You'll then have to think about the management of that business.

Will the original founder, owner, or staff stay on? Or will you have to take over the business and manage it? Is it a business you know something about? If the need arose, would you be able to manage it successfully on your own? What are your skills? Are they in the domain of the product or service that the company provides? Or are they in the area of business management? Personnel management? Marketing? Would you know enough about the results each aspect of the business should achieve to hold the appropriate people's feet to the fire? Are you prepared to take the risks that still remain? There will be many risks. Businesses are not static. They and the economic environment that surrounds them can change at the drop of a hat or the utterance of a politician.

Aggressive competition, the loss of a key management person, a marketing misstep, a sustained downswing in the economy, a public relations gaffe, and product obsolescence are but a few of the host of things that can torpedo a business.

The rewards of owning a business are considerable, but there are still plenty of risks, not the least of which are those revolving around liability and litigation—especially in today's world.

Each step you take to decrease risk decreases your reward at the same time. But you're still looking at the real benefits of adding value to create money and wealth, which is what a business does.

Perhaps it would be worthwhile to share the risk and the management responsibility with a partner or partners. Whatever money and skills you don't bring to the table, maybe other individuals could.

If you take on a partner or partners, however, you take on additional risks. Many partnerships just don't work out because too much disagreement develops over management or finance issues, or over the direction the company should take. Besides, taking on partners still doesn't remove the risk of litigation. Don't forget that as a partner you can be sued for everything you own, not just for what you have invested in the company.

If you want to share the business risks *and* eliminate the risk of liability, the answer is the corporation. With a corporation you can own the business or a part of it, share the risks, and limit your liability to just the extent of your ownership. This is by far the safest way to harness the ability of a business to add value and create wealth—your wealth. And owning an already-successful corporation will probably swing the odds around to your favor.

Evaluating the Business

So what's your desired corporation worth? You need to figure out a way to determine how much to pay for it.

First of all, you need to hire a competent accountant or analyst to look at the books. You wouldn't want to just take anyone's word that the company's strong. And you would want to make sure that the books have been audited. These things require a competent and honest professional.

You then need to look at the value of the machinery and property that the business owns, knocking off something for wear and tear and obsolescence. And you want to know whether the business is profitable and to ensure that it doesn't owe more money than it can comfortably afford to pay out of income. All of this comes from the company's financial statements, which you'll find reduced to their simplest terms in Chapter 4.

All of the previously mentioned notwithstanding, the most important determination you need to make is an assessment of how profitable the business can be for you. The bottom line (quite literally) is an evaluation of how quickly you'll get your investment back and start making money yourself. Whether you put the profit back in your pocket or let the business retain it, you'll start making money only after the business has recovered the cost of your original investment.

Negotiating the Price

You'll need to know how much of a profit the business makes each year, and you'll negotiate a price that is some multiple of that. Depending upon the kind of business, there are rules of thumb that suggest what conventional wisdom considers to be a fair multiple. Some businesses are typically valued at five times their earnings, and others at only three. There's no hard-and-fast rule beyond fair market value: the price at which there is a willing seller and a willing buyer. But whatever the price that is paid for a business, it translates into a multiple of the company's profits.

If you want to buy someone else's business and assume all of the responsibilities for running it as well as its risks and liabilities, multiples of three to five times the annual profit are about par for the course. And you will wind up paying something over and above the sticker price in the form of sweat equity: You will be doing the work and handling the responsibilities yourself.

Let's say that you are willing to pay three times last year's profit for a company that is capable of producing that profit year after year, a somewhat conventional multiple. After three years, you will have recovered your investment, and from then on everything will be gravy.

However, just think of what would happen if the profits were growing each year before your purchase instead of just remaining the same. Certainly the price that you'd expect to pay for the business would be higher, because it would be a much more valuable business with which to start. You would probably be willing to pay as much as five or six times last year's profit if it would still take you only three years to recover your investment and start making money. Thus, a fair multiple of profits is, in a sense, a measure of time: "How long will it take me to recover my investment?"

When you look at a business that is successful, that is increasingly profitable and is well managed by a team of accomplished professionals, and that will insulate you from the business's risks and liabilities because of its status as a corporation, you must expect—and will be willing—to pay a whole lot more.

To sum up, each of the levels of business participation I've described represents a reduction in risk, but it also represents an increase in the price of participation. To enjoy the greatest reward with the least risk, you should own a corporation—or a share of one and thus share the risk by sharing ownership with other investors. You would limit your liability to just the value of your investment. Your ownership would be based upon the amount of stock that you hold in the corporation, and you wouldn't have to worry about losing your home if someone sued the business. You would hire or retain the management that's capable of running your company successfully. And you would then reap your share of the profits.

If you could buy such a company, or an interest in it, and recover your investment from its profits within five years, your purchase price wouldn't be too much to pay. As you will see, my goal is to help you not just to recover your money in five years, but to double it. Surprisingly enough, the goal is an achievable one.

Owning Stock

A share of *common stock* represents part ownership of a corporation whose stock you have purchased. It entitles you to a "piece of the action." It gives you all of the benefits of outright ownership with few of the risks.

As an owner, you're entitled to a fractional share—a small fraction, to be sure—of the profits of that business, and you own a portion of its assets. Even if the company goes belly-up, you will receive a share of whatever value of the company might remain after its debts have been paid off.

If you own stock in a larger company that isn't growing or is growing only modestly, you will likely receive at least a portion of your profit in dividends. But that's not the most desirable option unless you're past retirement age and want to invest strictly for the income. Even then, there are compelling arguments against investing in such companies. I'll talk a little about the disadvantages later.

If, however, you own stock in a company whose profits grow every year, then you will probably not see any cash because your money will be plowed back into the company, showing up only as increased value. Until you sell your interest in the company, you won't be able to put that portion of its profit in the bank. Nor, by the way, will you have to pay taxes on it.

Only when you sell your interest to someone else will you realize the gain and pay the taxes. And because the company's profits will have grown, the price you can demand and receive for your interest in the company will have grown as well.

As a technamental investor you are going to select only world-class companies that have excellent track records and are still growing. (Chapter 6 goes into detail about the kinds of companies you should look for and how to find them). You'll find these companies listed on the New York Stock Exchange, the American Exchange, or the NASDAQ (National Association of Securities Dealers Automated Quotations), an electronic, "virtual" exchange.

Companies that are listed on these exchanges typically sell for many more times their profits than do those just getting started. The principle is the same, however. Ownership of companies that have gone well past the risk threshold will cost multiples upwards of 10, 15, or more. In fact, when the first edition of this book was written, there were some companies that were selling for multiples of more than 100! If a multiple is a measure of how long it will take to recover the investment, you can already appreciate the fact that those who would pay that many times the company's profit either are expecting to live well beyond the normal life span or are very foolish indeed!

Diversification: Spreading the Risk

Putting all your eggs in one basket has never been smart. No matter how good the basket is, something can always happen to it. The last step in understanding why you should buy common stock is to understand the final reduction of risk.

If one business will give you a good return, why not invest in small pieces of a bunch of businesses? If you study companies—an easy job, as you will shortly discover—you'll be able to eliminate from consideration all of the companies that are below average. You can then assemble a collection—a *portfolio*—of above-average companies that will perform better than the rest. And because you have your eggs in a variety of baskets, you will not have to worry about all of the risks that could blow a single company out of the water.

This is called *diversification*, and it's the final reason why ownership of common stocks is the place to be. When you own a few shares of a variety of above-average companies, you reduce your risk while retaining all of the benefits of owning businesses—those wonderful engines for adding value and making money.

31

Investing vs. Playing the Market

The expression "playing the market" should be your first clue that this is something you don't want to do with your money. If you want to play, then you can certainly get the same kind of rush in the stock market that you get at the tables in Las Vegas or Atlantic City, and you can enjoy the same success that most people who play those tables enjoy: none. When you play the market, the odds are very much against you. So if you think that this book will help you play more successfully, you're reading the wrong book!

There is a basic difference between what I propose and what many unfortunate folks do. I suggest that you earn your money by participating in a business, not bet that you can make a killing by finding someone who will pay a lot more for the stock than you did. When you invest, you depend upon the successful businesses you have chosen to add value and create money.

Don't kid yourself! Playing the market is gambling in its truest sense. The risks that a player takes are enormous because the rewards aren't based upon the orderly supply of products or services for which people are willing to pay a fair price. A player relies upon a variety of totally unpredictable events or occurrences, as does a gambler at the roulette table. This is the playground of the traders.

Stock was first issued for the sole purpose of allowing more than one individual to participate in a venture. Later a market sprang up that allowed people to sell their shares to others, and it created a new kind of share owner, one who likes to speculate by buying and selling shares. The dynamics of that market well suits those who are eager to get rich in a hurry.

Psychology has always played a major role as shares were bought out of greed and sold out of fear. Until recent years it wasn't difficult for unscrupulous people to manipulate the price of shares by planting fears or by spreading excessively optimistic stories. They would then buy below or sell above the real value of the shares, before the enterprise itself was able to add to the shares' value.

Today the stock market does a roaring business while traders watch the minute-to-minute movement of the prices and frantically sell or buy shares when they move up or down by only a few cents.

The BFS/STS School of Speculation

Ask the average person what she thinks of the stock market and she will probably say it's scary. Everyone has either lost money on the stock market or can recite some horror story about someone she knows who has. As is the case with those who play the lottery, only a chosen few among traders who make the big bucks; the great majority have been burned.

Except for the professionals, the stock market today is made up largely of folks who have no concept of the fact that they're really buying a company rather than merely buying its stock. These investors hold to what I call the *BFS/STS School of Speculation*.

"BFS/STS" means "buy from a sucker, sell to a sucker." What is their methodology? It's simple. You have to first buy the stock from some poor sucker who doesn't know its true value as well as you do. And then you have to turn around and sell it to some other poor sucker who doesn't know its true value either, or else he wouldn't buy it from you for the price you're asking.

What chance do you think the average investor—or you, for that matter—has of not being the sucker on at least one end of that transaction, if not both? Slim to none! If there is no rational means of determining the reasonable value of a stock, the only thing that provides the opportunity for people to sell their stocks at a profit is the presence of someone who is similarly unenlightened. The street has cynically called this phenomenon by another name: the "Greater Fool Theory." Each buyer admits to being a fool but relies on the next buyer to be yet a greater one.

On the other hand, if you buy stock in a growing company, having determined (in the fashion that you'll shortly learn) that the stock is worth a certain multiple of the previous year's profit, you'll have paid a fair price for it. Over the long term you'll see profits grow, and the value of the company will grow right along with them. As time passes, assuming the multiple you paid was reasonable, another buyer will be quite willing to pay as high a multiple as you did—perhaps higher. The same multiple times twice the profit means twice the price; your investment's value will have doubled. Long-term investing is not a gamble, nor does it depend on finding a "greater fool" to take your holdings off your hands.

33

Why Invest for the Long Term?

The decision is yours to make. At this point, you may still prefer the rush that goes with betting on the long shots and you'd rather ride the hare to the finish line than the tortoise. Just so you know what you're missing if you do, here are some of the benefits of doing it my way:

Pick Winners 4 out of 5 Times

Nearly a half century of experience with this methodology allows NAIC to boast that if you have done your homework diligently and conservatively, for every five stocks you pick, one will exceed your highest expectations, three will do about as you expected them to, and one will go down the tubes. This is called the *Rule of Five*, and you should keep it in mind when you worry about having some failures.

No one can predict when some calamity will befall a company. For example, not long ago a major food chain lost all of its high-level executives in an airplane crash. How could *anyone* have predicted that?

All kinds of risks can come without notice, but the odds are in your favor. If you do it right—and it's really not hard—you can enjoy an 80-percent success rate. That ain't too shabby!

Double Your Money Every 5 Years

If you're able to pick stocks that do you proud four out of five times, you can double your money every five years. With this "sure thing" philosophy, all you have to do is to watch the companies you've bought to make sure that, other than the occasional stumble that good management is allowed once in a while, your companies continue to perform as you expected. If their growth continues substantially as you anticipated, then the price of their shares will do the same over the long term, despite the fluctuations that occur every day.

Consider this: The S&P 500 is a dollar-weighted index of some 500 stocks that have been selected as representative of their industries and that meet certain quality criteria. Since its inception, the S&P 500 has produced an average annual return of around 10 percent. This means that, if you had bought all 500 of these companies, you would have increased the value of your investments by 10 percent after holding them for a year. This hasn't been the case every year, but the average has been around 10 percent.

Because this performance is for an *average* of 500 companies, doesn't it stand to reason that, if you can eliminate the below-average companies and pick just a few of the very best, your performance might easily be again half as good?

As a technamental investor, you will look for a return on your portfolio of 15 percent, which, compounded annually, will double your money every five years. (*Compounding* simply means that each year the earnings from the previous year are added to the value of the investment, and growth is then calculated on the new value.) Doubling the value of your investment in five years is quite achievable. There are hundreds of thousands of folks just like you out there who are doing it all the time!

Maintain Your Portfolio Painlessly

How would you like to be so confident in your investments that you check their performance only once a month, or every three months, or even once a year? Do you think that's smart—or even possible?

This is one of the great benefits of buying the company and not the stock. If you subscribe to the BFS/STS School of Speculation, you have to watch every movement of the price, the thing you're most concerned about. The price changes every minute that the exchange on which the stock trades is open. In fact, the price can even change during the night when the exchange is not open, which can drive traders nuts. Moreover, prices can fluctuate by as much as 50 percent above and below their averages during the course of a year. As a trader, you're afraid to miss a trick!

Long-term investors know that the price will fluctuate in the short term for a variety of reasons, most of them irrelevant. They don't have to worry about those fluctuations in price because they know one simple fact (and I'll repeat this later because it's important): *Changes in price that are not caused by changes in the fundamentals (sales, profits, and so forth) are transient. What goes up will come down, and what goes down will come back up.* Because the price of a stock over the long term is directly related to the company's profits, there's really no point in watching the price zigzag as it does every minute of every hour of every weekday. If you want to make money, you'll invest, not gamble. Watching the short-term fluctuations in the price is hardly different from sitting at the roulette table. It may be exciting, but it's not likely to beat your day job!

Everyone's a Winner!

This point may be redundant, but it's worth repeating. Technamental investing—this long-term, buy-and-hold, fundamental investment philosophy—produces no losers. If you perform the simple tasks related to studying a company before you buy it, and if you diversify enough so that the Rule of Five gives you at least 80-percent odds of being satisfied, you can't lose! Nor will you need to find a sucker to sell to because, when you're ready to sell something, you'll offer it at a fair value. Not only will you win, but the person who buys the stock from you at a fair price will make out just as well.

Defer Taxes

As a bonus benefit, don't forget that there is no tax on your gain until you sell your stock.

There are only two main reasons for selling your shares: if a company's fundamentals (that is, its operational performance) deteriorate so much that the company no longer meets your expectations, or if you need or want the money. (There's a third, unusual, occasion that I'll talk about in Chapter 12.)

Otherwise, let that company simply generate those profits, plow them back into the business, and make the value of your holdings increase year after year as its earnings grow. And defer paying taxes on those unrealized gains until you're ready to sell.

Although you can *defer* the payment of taxes, there are only two circumstances that allow you to *avoid* paying taxes on gains: your death or the loss of your gains. Neither of these alternatives is palatable.

Traders, who are in and out of the market buying low and selling high, have to pay a tax on every cent of profit they earn—when they earn it. If they have to pay 20 percent of their gain, that's 20 percent less that they can reinvest and earn money on.

You may ask, "What about an IRA or a 401(k), where I don't have to pay taxes until I take out the money?" These investment vehicles can certainly be good when you want to move your money from one company to another that has a greater potential without incurring a tax liability. And the 401(k) is a great boon to many people who wouldn't otherwise discipline themselves to invest. What's more, if you're fortunate enough to have a program where the company contributes matching funds to your investment program, you're already making 100 percent on your investment, and that's hard to beat anywhere else!

The biggest benefit of tax-deferred investments is that you can reinvest money you would otherwise have had to pay out in taxes. And the money earned on that reinvestment can continue to grow without being taxed until later.

There's no free lunch, though. You will pay a substantial cost for this benefit later on. The taxes on your gains when you finally do take out your money are paid not at the capital gains rate, which can be as low as 5 percent, but at the full rate that applies to ordinary income (although by the time you reach retirement age, your tax rate will probably have come down some).

At this writing, the highest personal tax rate is more than three times the capital gains rate! So unless Congress acts in a way that is quite out of character, you will have to do a great deal of optimizing to make up for paying almost triple the taxes.

Clearly, the least costly gains are the gains in a non-tax-deferred portfolio. And it's a pleasure to watch the value of your holdings increase year after year without having to pay a tax on those increases in value.

If You're Retired and Don't Have a "Long Term"

Finally, I'd like to address the question of how this long-term philosophy can be of benefit to people in the "third third," people who are in their golden years, when it's time to make use of the funds they've accumulated for this time of their life.

My counsel to anyone at any age is to pretend that you're going to live forever. Not only will this give you a happier outlook from the time you wake up until the time you go back to sleep, but it will provide you with a better investment plan.

No matter how you slice it, a 15-percent return is better than a 6-percent return—more than twice as good—and you will be able to endure a lot of leaner years if you have more than twice the accumulation of wealth when times are good.

Since the early 1940s, when World War II brought the Depression to an end, there has never been a long-term catastrophe in the stock market. Even in the worst of times, good companies continue to earn, and many stocks buck the trend. To be sure, some of the weaker companies with poor management fold, but the well-managed, strong companies quickly scoop up their market share and life goes on.

Focus on investing in growth companies for the long term and, if the time arises when you need to take cash out of your account, sell off portions of your losers—the ones whose sales and profit growth is sluggish, not necessarily the ones whose prices are down.

This will assure you that when the market comes back up, which it surely will, you'll have a portfolio of winners. Have faith that the companies you own a piece of will perform well in the long term and so, therefore, will your investments. And gloat as you continue to rack up 15-percent years while your contemporaries are pulling down 6 percent and paying the taxes on it every month.

Let's Take Stock of The Reasons You Should Take Stock

➤ You can create wealth only by adding value to resources or by providing a service of value.

➤ Only investments in active businesses are capable of adding value.

➤ Owning a business, though very rewarding, is expensive and risky; but owning shares in a variety of successful businesses eliminates most of the risk while retaining most of the reward.

> Buying the stock of quality growth companies and holding it for the long term provides substantial, predictable returns.

> Short-term trading (BFS/STS) is unpredictable and stacks the odds against you, because it relies upon winning at some loser's expense and because there's no assurance that you won't be the loser.

> The benefits of long-term investing include carefree portfolio maintenance, the potential to double your money every five years, the deferment of taxes, and the fact that there are rarely any losers.

Finally, let's review the simple math that makes this method work:

1. Assume that 15 times earnings is a fair multiple for a good company and that the company earned a dollar per share last year.

2. You will therefore pay $15 for the stock.

3. In five years, the earnings will have grown to $2 per share.

4. At 15 times earnings, the price will then be $30.

The value of your investment will have doubled—in five years!

Hopefully you're satisfied with the logic behind this investing approach and can see its advantages.

Next, let's dispel any doubts you might have about whether you can be successful.

CHAPTER 3

Dispelling the Myths

There's a tremendous mystique out there about investing in stocks. So let's blow it away!

"Only people on the inside have access to the secret knowledge, which is surrounded by a huge, nearly impenetrable wall. The wall prevents anyone but the insiders from knowing enough to invest successfully on their own."

Baloney! It's a myth!

"Without a degree in finance or the letters MBA or CFA after your name, you just can't begin to know enough about business or the stock market to succeed."

So the professional community would have you believe. It's all nonsense!

Just think of all of the people in the investment business who have a stake in convincing you that you can't do it yourself!

For instance, where would the brokers be if you could make your own decisions without their help? Why, they'd be reduced to just taking your phone calls and executing your orders. Hardly more than you could do for yourself on the Internet—and you can do it after working hours to boot!

Money managers, mutual fund managers, analysts who make their recommendations in the avalanche of newsletters that you could be buried under if you let them just send the trial subscriptions, and all of the clerks, secretaries, computer technicians, chauffeurs (some of them make really big bucks), and the others who support them are all interested in keeping you in the dark because your ignorance is their bread, butter, and caviar.

Well, this is certainly an intimidating business. Just think of all of the things they know that you don't. And still they rarely do better than the market average! Well, I've got news for you. As with the proverbial bumble-bee that floats through the air even though aeronautical engineers have proclaimed that she can't possibly fly, there are literally millions of folks out there, from grandparents to little school kids, who successfully ignore that claim and invest successfully in stocks. And you can too!

And it's not because the folks who do so are smart and the professionals are stupid. They're not at all stupid—at least not most of them. One problem is that they are working with money that's not their own. In order to avoid the liability that can go with handling other people's money, most mutual funds, banks, insurance companies, and money management firms have adopted a very conservative set of constraints. And the Securities and Exchange Commission (SEC) has also laid down some laws to protect the public. These prevent the pros from doing some of the things that you can do.

Some of the rules are so conservative as to be ludicrous; others have some merit to them but still stand in the way of excellent performance.

One of the biggest restraints on professional success is the way the professionals are rated. Their peers and the financial press judge the fund managers each quarter on the basis of what stocks are in their portfolios. So every three months there's a "rush to flush" stocks that are out of favor and replace them with "hot" ones. This vanity can be very costly to the fund's shareholders.

Peter Lynch Says We Can Do It

Without question, the most celebrated professional investor in history has been Peter Lynch. There have been others, such as Warren Buffett and Sir John Templeton, who have made immense personal fortunes and who have shared their investment methods with the world. But the highest-profile investor, the consummate professional, is Peter Lynch.

Lynch has served as an inspiration to me and to millions of others who were initially bamboozled by the belief that we can't do a good job of investing in common stocks without help.

As the manager of history's arguably most successful mutual fund, Fidelity's Magellan, Lynch shepherded the fund's holdings from a relatively small $475 million or so to $9 billion in just over 11 years, from 1977 through 1989, when his book was published.

Lynch's wonderful *One Up on Wall Street* is a must-read. You should read it if only for the inspiration that he and his coauthor, John Rothchild, have given the world in this first light-hearted primer for bamboozled would-be investors. In the first paragraph of the first chapter, Lynch writes, *"Any normal person using the customary three percent of his brain can pick stocks as well, or better than, the average Wall Street expert."* Take this to heart! How much simpler can it be said? And to whom can you look for greater credibility? There you have it: the quintessential professional telling you that you can do it. And you can!

NAIC Has Proven We Can Do It

More than five million investors have passed through the portals of NAIC since it was founded in 1951. Most learn and then leave once they have acquired the basics. But there's a solid core of several thousand volunteers who form the nucleus of NAIC's educational establishment. Beyond that, more than 200,000 individuals, including members of investment clubs, are active NAIC members. (If you would like to find out more about NAIC, point your browser to *www.better-investing.org*.)

Thousands upon thousands of NAIC members do better than the average professional every day. And even the worst-performing NAIC members don't do nearly so badly as some professionals do.

Speaking of inspiration, track records, and publicity, how about the famed Beardstown Ladies? You probably remember when they burst upon the scene—an investment club composed of some 16 ladies from that small Illinois town. Ranging in age from a youthful 41 to more than twice that age, the Beardstown Ladies learned how to select stocks and made money in the stock market.

You probably also remember the publicity when it appeared that their track record wasn't nearly as good as they had thought it was. Through an honest mistake they had miscalculated their returns. They had acquired a computer program to do their club's accounting, and after entering the data into the program they thought the 23.4-percent return the program reported was for the previous nine years rather than for only the two years actually calculated.

How the financial press and the pros crowed! Here was proof positive that common people—and certainly an investment club made up of women averaging 70 years of age—could not do better than they. But they had missed the point: By using some very homespun, commonsense rules, the Beardstown Ladies had actually succeeded.

As it turned out, the Ladies' annual return since the inception of their club was a very respectable 15.3 percent—this time verified by hawkeyed auditors. This is as much as we would hope for. And there are many folks out there similar to you who are investing successfully because the Beardstown Ladies inspired them to do it!

Be like the bumblebee and pay no attention to the experts who tell you that you can't do it. Do it anyway!

I Say You Can Do It—and *Easily*

So don't take Peter Lynch's word for it. Maybe you figure that he's in a different league and can't possibly be talking to you.

Be skeptical about NAIC's track record if you like. After all, if you haven't personally talked to all of those folks out there, you don't really know whom you can believe.

Perhaps you may even join the legion of cynics who can't look beyond the Beardstown Ladies' mistake and see the plain truth in their story and the moral to be learned from it.

But you certainly can't be enough of a skeptic to doubt your own common sense, can you?

I'm not only telling you that you can invest successfully; I'm telling you that you can do it easily, that it's well within your reach to understand the principles, no matter what level of education you have—or haven't— achieved.

Here I'm going to summarize what the rest of this book will tell you in much greater detail. If it makes good sense, if it seems logical enough to you and sounds reasonably easy, then you're well on your way!

Here's All There Is to It

To successfully pick good stocks, there are only two things that you need to determine about a company:

1. Whether the company is a good-quality business worthy of your interest as an investor.

2. Whether the company's stock is selling for a reasonable price. (No matter how good the company, it can still be a poor investment if the price is too high.)

The 2 Tests of Quality

There are only two things that you have to look at to determine whether the company is of good enough quality.

1. *Growth of revenue and earnings.* The first consideration is the company's track record. How successful has the company been in selling an increasing number of its products or services? And how successful has management been in converting those growing sales into profits for the shareholders?

2. *Efficiency.* The second consideration is management's ability to sustain that track record. How capable is management of controlling costs?

Don't worry at this point if you aren't sure exactly what these terms mean. They're defined quite simply in the next chapter.

Using the tools of technamental analysis described in Chapters 7, 8, and 9, you'll be able to actually see a company's growth and efficiency quite plainly.

The 2 Tests of Value

When you're satisfied that the company would be a good one to own, *and only then,* you will assess two more factors to determine whether the price you must pay for its stock is reasonable. They are:

1. The *potential return* that you can expect on your investment. Is it sufficient at the price you're being asked to pay?

2. The *risk* that you must take. Is it reasonable for the reward?

You'll learn how to assess these criteria in Chapter 10.

If your company passes these two tests of value, there is an 80-percent chance that you have found a winner.

Let's Take Stock of Your Chances for Success

> ➤ In spite of the many obvious reasons that people want you to believe you can't be a successful investor without the help of investment professionals, abundant evidence exists to support the fact that you can! The consummate professional Peter Lynch says so. NAIC's five decades of success bear it out. And the simple logic of the approach makes plenty of sense.

> ➤ The two measurable criteria to determine the quality of a potential investment are the company's *growth* and management's *efficiency*, its ability to sustain that growth.

> ➤ The two measurable criteria to determine whether the stock is selling for a reasonable price are its potential reward and the accompanying risk.

> ➤ At least four out of five companies that pass the simple tests that measure these criteria should prove to be good investments for the long term.

And you can become wealthy with such a track record.

CHAPTER 4

Learning the Language

You're about to become a fundamental analyst, and that's the best kind! All of the acknowledged great investors are or have been fundamental analysts. So you'll join the ranks of the Peter Lynches, the Warren Buffets, the Sir John Templetons, and the Grahams and the Dodds.

But if you read any of the books the successful professional fundamental analysts have written, although you may be inspired and excited, you're apt to be left with an inexplicable sense of intellectual discomfort. Why? Because there are few, if any, that will tell you in plain language how to make decisions.

The reason for this is that they include a confusing variety of ratios and measurements that, although useful to those who manage the companies, are not all that valuable to the investor.

Trust me. You don't have to worry about any of this stuff. I'm not pretending to be as experienced or as knowledgeable as any of these respected authors, but I am telling you emphatically that you can succeed even if you don't know any more than I do.

At the end of this chapter, after you've learned the only 10 very simple things you *do* need to know, I'll talk about those things you don't, and why they won't help you. And, at the end of the book, in Appendix A, I'll even provide you with a glossary of those terms, tell you how to calculate them, and give you a little insight into what they mean so you can impress your broker or your friends.

Most important: When you finish this book, you'll have some clear direction and be able to make good decisions. And, although this method isn't foolproof—you won't be right all of the time—it is predictable and you'll probably be right 80 percent of the time. And that's enough to make you very successful.

So let's get down to business.

First, What Do You Need to Know?

The first step in learning how to evaluate companies and their stock is to understand the terms that are used—the ones that you *do* have to know. You'll need to understand the language that's commonly used to refer to the things you'll examine and evaluate. What's good about learning this "foreign language" is that there are only 10 terms that you need to know.

The rest of the fancy expressions to which I referred are not required. This is because there's a sharp distinction between what you need to know to understand the company's financial results and the tools the company's management uses to produce those results.

Think about it. You don't have to know what's going on under the hood of your car to drive to the store! You don't need to know the micrometer settings for the spark plug gaps, the specifications for the fuel/air mixture in the carburetor, or anything else about the host of other things that make your car run properly. All you need to know is that it starts right up, it runs smoothly, and it stops when you put on the brake. If any of these things doesn't go right, you can simply tell the garage mechanic in commonsense terms what he needs to know to start diagnosing and solving the problem. That's *his* job.

Fortunately, there's a whole lot more oversight to protect you from unscrupulous business managers than there is to protect you from unscrupulous garage mechanics—especially nowadays. In fact, never has it been safer to invest in common stocks, considering the political focus and pressure on corporate governance, accounting practices, conflicts of interest in the securities industry, and management of mutual funds that started and has crescendoed since the lid blew off Enron in late 2001.

When you look at a company, you need only to be able to tell how well it runs. You have neither the responsibility nor the authority to tell someone to fix it if it's not running right. You can't hire, train, or fire management. All you can do is find another company with which to replace it. Therefore, it's about as important for you to dig into those other terms and tools as it would be for you to know the amount and viscosity of the residual oil in your engine's crankcase!

Later, perhaps, after you've digested all of the basics and are comfortable with the use of the tools *you* need to work with, your curiosity may lead you to explore some of those more cryptic things. That's the right time to dig deeper, not when you can be easily distracted into thinking that there's more to this exercise than there really is.

Even then, if you were to learn everything that a professional has learned about management's tools of the trade, their utility to you would be minimal. If you aren't in on all of the insider information that a company's management has at its disposal—and you won't be—you still won't be able to put those tools to much practical use. And even if you were to foresee a problem because you were using those tools, you simply wouldn't be able to predict what management would do when it discovered the problem itself, or whether it had already put some fix in motion. Besides, management can—in fact must—focus only on its own company. You are the "owner" of many companies.

So let's concentrate only on the things that you need to know and forget about the rest for now.

The first term you already know about because we've discussed it at some length already. However, just to be sure, let's review what a *share of stock* is.

Share of Stock

It's absolutely imperative that you're clear on the fact that a share of stock is just what the name implies: a share, a piece of the action of an enterprise. It's not a kind of currency. It's not like a baseball card that has value in and of itself and can or should be traded. Its purpose is to give the person who owns it the right to share in the profit of the company that issues it.

It provides evidence that you, along with many others, have an ownership claim to the company's value and even have a right to help set the company's policy should you choose to exercise that right. When you purchase a number of shares of stock, you're purchasing a fractional interest in a company, and that fraction, however small, represents your percentage of ownership of the company. We'll talk about how to assess the value of your ownership shortly.

The next eight items are also quite elementary. So elementary, in fact, that they can be applied just as readily to Lucy's Lemonade Stand as to General Motors.

When you study any company, you will want to look at two things about it: how it has operated over a period of time and what its condition is at the end of that time. Although as a rule Lucy wouldn't issue financial statements for her lemonade stand, she very well could.

To report on her lemonade stand's *performance*, Lucy might issue an *income statement* that says, "I made $10 this week." To report on its *condition* at the end of the week, she might issue a *balance sheet* that says, "Now I have $20."

Companies issue these reports every three months (each *quarter*) with a major report being issued each year showing the results for the entire *fiscal year*. I'll tell you later where you may find these reports. For now, let's just look at what's in them.

The company's performance is what "feeds" its condition. The more money a company earns, the better its condition. The income statement therefore feeds the balance sheet, and the items on each are quite similar.

I have somewhat oversimplified the notion that some things are "good" and others "bad." Expenses, for example, are good because the money is usually well spent and what it buys is necessary to make money. However, for our purposes, anything that benefits the company by having more of it is good; anything that will make a company better off by having less of it is bad.

The Income Statement

Because your biggest concern is the company's operation, you're going to want to look at the income statement first. Its purpose is to chronicle the company's performance.

Though there may be as many as 50 items or more on the income statement, only four are important to you. These four items represent categories that consolidate or sum up all of the other items that can appear on an income statement.

Sales/Revenue

The first item is *sales*. For Lucy, this figure represents all of the money she takes in over the counter for her lemonade. For a corporation, it's all of the compensation that it receives for the goods or services that it provides.

For some companies the word *revenue* is more appropriate because this more encompassing word goes beyond the marketing of goods or services and takes into account such odd things as rental income, interest income, and so on. For our purposes, however, we'll make *sales* and *revenue* interchangeable. Whatever the company brings in is sales. This is what a company would call its *top line*, meaning that this is the first thing that you'll find at the top of the income statement.

For Lucy's Lemonade Stand, sales would include one item only: lemonade. But a large manufacturing company may market many products or services. So the company will want to keep track of how many dollars come from each source so it can analyze what sells and what doesn't. These breakdowns are important for management's guidance but not for us. We're interested only in the total revenue. Keep this in mind when you look at a complicated annual report. You should just look for totals. (See Figure 4.1 on page 52.)

Not all sales are paid for at the time the sale is made or the product delivered. Most companies bill their customers for goods or services and are paid at a later date. These sales are still included in the sales figure because delivery has been made and the obligation has been incurred by the purchaser. The income statement will make no distinction between transactions with delayed payment and transactions for cash. That difference shows up later on the balance sheet.

51

ABC Company
Income Statement
for Year Ending May 31, 2004

	2004
Sales	
Net sales...	$ 757,414
Cost of sales..	229,727
Gross profit.....................................	527,687
Expenses	
Selling, general, and administrative expense.........	236,065
Research and development expense....................	35,472
Depreciation..	29,500
Special charge...	11,650
Total operating and fixed expense....................	312,687
Operating income..................................	215,000
Other income, net..................................	14,696
Profit	
Profit before income taxes...............................	229,696
Provision for income taxes..........................	80,623
Net profit to shareholders............................	149,073
Earnings per share:	
Basic..	$1.34
Diluted..	1.32
Shares used in the computation of earnings per share:	
Basic..	111,509
Diluted...	112,582
Cash dividends paid per common share................	$ .12

Figure 4.1. Income Statement

Expenses

The second item you're interested in is *expenses*. For obvious reasons, you would consider these "bad." The higher your expenses are, the worse off you are.

For Lucy, the cost of lemons and sugar is about as complicated as it gets. For a manufacturer, expenses will range from the cost of raw materials to the costs of a product's fabrication and delivery.

These *variable* expenses are known as the *cost of goods sold*, or COGS. Variable costs will vary with the number of units made. The more units produced, the higher the cost.

Fixed expenses, items such as rent, salaries, interest on mortgages, and so on, are items that remain essentially the same regardless of how many units of a product are made.

Taxes are an expense as well. Taxes vary with the amount of profit, so they are considered separately in the income statement.

Again, we don't need to keep track of these distinctions—at least for the moment. We need only be concerned with the total.

Profit

If we subtract the expenses from the sales, we come up with the *profit*, our third term. Profit is obviously "good." Profit is what you have left after paying your expenses. It's what Lucy's been standing behind that table in the hot sun all week for. And it's what you, as a shareholder of a company, are entitled to a part of. It's the result of adding value and creating wealth. It's what the enterprise is all about.

Profit is not obscene, as some would have you believe. It's what the company uses to hire more people, buy more machines to work with, and create more jobs. It's what you want your company to make for you—and what it will ultimately use to reward you for allowing it to use your money.

This simple definition of profit leads us to the next term, to the figure that makes your company's performance more "personal." It converts the company's performance to a value that you can apply to your own share of the company.

Earnings per Share

When you divide the profit by the number of shares of stock that you and all of your fellow shareholders own, you will have calculated *earnings per share*, or EPS—a figure that represents just how much of that profit is attributable to each share of stock. This number is what's known as the *bottom line*, and it will, logically enough, be found at the very bottom of the income statement. From here on, I'll use earnings or EPS to refer to earnings per share.

If you were Lucy's dad or mom and agreed to fund her venture in return for half of the proceeds, your single share of Lucy's enterprise would be worth half of her profit. Your half of the profit would equal the EPS. In a large company, your share is only a small fraction of all of the ownership, so you'll receive a lot less than half of the profit. Your share of that company's earnings is the EPS multiplied by the number of shares you own. If the company had issued a million shares and had earned a million dollars during the past three months, each of your shares would have earned $1 for you. If you had a hundred shares, your holdings would have earned you $100.

However, you wouldn't receive a check for that $100. If this company were to pay you and all of the other stockholders all of the earnings that your stock entitled you to in dividends, the company would go nowhere and you would have no reason to be interested in it as an investment. It's the portion of the profit that is retained by the company that fuels its growth, and it's that growth that's going to make you the money on your investment. In effect, your company is reinvesting your earnings back into itself, which is the best place for them to go, assuming the company's track record comes up to your standards. The most promising growth companies are usually those that retain all of their earnings and pay no dividends.

If the company is a very large, mature company, it will reward its stockholders by paying them a portion of the earnings while retaining the rest for growth. These larger companies have increased their revenues to the point where spectacular growth is no longer possible, so it's appropriate that they reward their shareholders with dividends.

Large, mature companies are not the ones that will usually make the most money for you, but some mature companies of especially high quality, such as General Electric (GE), can provide stability to your portfolio and certainly have a place there.

You'll find most of the information you'll need in the company's income statement. As a long-term, growth/value investor, you are mostly interested in finding companies whose ability to produce earnings is sufficient to keep those earnings growing into the future. And as you now know, it's the growth of earnings that increases the value of your stock when you go to sell it to someone else down the road.

The company's track record, on which you base your judgment, is documented by not just one, but rather a series of income statements. You will extract just the basic information from each to analyze how rapidly and steadily sales and earnings have grown from year to year and quarter to quarter. Simple enough?

The Balance Sheet

Most of us are blessed with two eyes, each of which has a slightly different perspective, giving us depth perception so that we can judge distance, size, and movement much more accurately than we could with a single eye.

The balance sheet affords you a second perspective of a company. It gives you a picture of the substance of the company and the value of your ownership of it.

As with the income statement, the balance sheet (see Figure 4.2 on page 56) documents some very basic items that can be classified simply as "good" or "bad."

Assets

Assets are everything the company owns.

If Lucy came to you and asked you to invest in her lemonade stand, you might give her $20 to buy lemons and sugar, a pitcher, some cups, and a table to put them on. All of these, including any change she might have left after her purchases, would be assets. Assets are the things that the company owns and that it uses to add value, make money, and, closer to

55

ABC Company
Balance Sheet
Year Ending 5/31/04

Assets
Current assets:

Cash and cash equivalents	$ 129,359
Investments	60,078
Accounts and notes receivable, less allowance for doubtful receivables (1999 - $4,883 and 1998 - $5,957)	215,034
Refundable income taxes	31,308
Inventories	205,238
Prepaid expenses and other	40,691
Total current assets	681,708

Property, plant, and equipment:

Land and improvements	13,544
Buildings and improvements	92,396
Machinery and equipment	159,070
	265,010
Less, accumulated depreciation	96,137
Property, plant, and equipment, net	168,873
Investments	146,859
Intangible assets, net of accumulated amortization (1999 - $18,096 and 1998 - $14,427)	7,665
Excess acquisition costs over fair value of acquired net assets, net of accumulated amortization (1999 - $15,816 and 1998 - $11,102)	47,861
Other assets	14,990
Total assets	**$ 1,067,956**

Liabilities and Shareholders' Equity
Current liabilities:

Short-term borrowings	$ 45,137
Accounts payable	27,676
Accrued income taxes	17,088
Accrued wages and commissions	19,596
Accrued insurance	9,197
Accrued litigation	55,000
Other accrued expenses	27,736
Total current liabilities	201,430
Deferred federal income taxes	9,565
Other liabilities	324
Total liabilities	**211,319**
Minority interest	80,690

Commitments and contingencies (Note L)

Shareholders' equity:

Preferred shares, $100 par value: Authorized 5 shares; none issued	
Common shares, without par value: Authorized 500,000 shares; issued and outstanding 1999 - 112,578 shares and 1998 - 112,043 shares	77,843
Additional paid-in capital	26,920
Retained earnings	687,828
Accumulated other comprehensive loss	(16,644)
Total shareholders' equity	**775,947**
Total liabilities and shareholders' equity	$ 1,067,956

Figure 4.2. The Balance Sheet

home, generate your earnings. Assets are generally classified as *liquid* or *fixed*. The $20 would have been a liquid asset; the nonexpendable items, such as the pitcher and table, would be fixed assets.

Such things as cash, factory buildings, machines, vehicles, postage stamps, and paper clips—all are assets. Some are more liquid than others; they are easier to spend because they are easier to convert to cash. Cash itself is the most liquid asset; money in a checking account is not far behind and is, in fact, easier to move around than currency.

All the money owed to the company by its customers at the end of the period, its *accounts receivable*, is an asset that is nearly as liquid as cash because, if the company is well managed and careful, the accounts receivable will soon be converted to cash. Other liquid assets are loans that the company has made, mortgages it owns, even stock in other companies in which management has invested spare cash so that it will earn something.

Machinery, vehicles, and other items that the company has purchased for its use are obviously less liquid because they are not nearly so easily converted to cash. Probably the least liquid of all of the fixed assets are land and the structures that sit on it.

You can lump all of the things the company owns into the single category called assets.

Liabilities

Liabilities are everything that the company owes. For obvious reasons, you would consider these "bad."

If you loan Lucy $20 instead of buying a piece of her action by becoming a shareholder, she incurs a liability. The good news for her enterprise is that after she pays you a fixed amount each week, she can keep all of the earnings above and beyond those payments for herself. The bad news is that no matter how many days it rains, she still has to make the payments every week.

Liabilities are recorded in the balance sheet in order of the length of the time the company has to repay them. Short-term liabilities such as *accounts payable*—the money the company owes for goods and services it has purchased and for short-term notes and loans—are called short-term liabilities, appropriately enough.

Long-term liabilities include such things as installment loans and mortgages on real estate. They also include bonds, debt instruments that must be repaid at the end of a fixed term and on which regular interest payments must be paid. Bonds constitute most of the long-term debt of companies that have funded some of their growth and asset acquisition by borrowing money instead of by issuing more stock to more shareholders.

When the company borrows money to acquire assets, it can benefit you as a shareholder because the increased profits that are generated by those additional assets are divided among fewer shares than they would have been if more shares had been issued to cover the cost of the assets. This is called *leverage*, another of those nifty management tools that you don't have to be concerned with.

As you know from common sense, borrowing can also be a problem for the company and its shareholders. When times are hard, a demanding creditor can put a company out of business, forcing it to sell all of its assets to pay off the debt. Hopefully that won't happen to any of the companies you own a piece of.

Equity

Equity is what you have left when you subtract the liabilities from the assets. It is the "live" part of the company that grows. What's more important, the equity of the company is a statement of the value of that company—what you own a piece of. And it is "good."

At the end of each period for which the income statement shows more income than expense, all profits that are not paid out to in dividends are retained—added to the equity of the company.

Equity can include not only the tangible difference between assets and liabilities, but a company can also own intangible things with real value such as brand recognition or customer goodwill. Any of these things can have a value attached and be a part of what you own as a stockholder. This kind of hard-to-wrap-your-arms-around value is part of a company's potential growth as well, and it is sometimes referred to as *franchise value*.

Book Value per Share

As with per share earnings, your portion of equity—the company's value—is determined by dividing the equity by the number of shares of stock issued. The result is called *book value*, or *book value per share*. From here on, I'll simply use book value to refer to book value per share.

To "personalize" it again, you can see just how much your part of the company is worth by multiplying the book value by the number of shares you own. Thus, if the company is worth $100 million and it has 1 million shares outstanding, each share is worth $100. If you own 100 shares, they would be worth $10,000 (exclusive of the value of their potential earnings growth) if the company were to liquidate its assets and pay its liabilities.

For you as a growth/value investor, book value is not of much importance. Heaven forbid you own stock in a company that has to liquidate its assets!

These eight terms: sales, expenses, profit, and earnings per share from the income statement; and assets, liabilities, equity, and book value from the balance sheet—all somewhat related—are all you need to know to understand how a company works. There is just one more term that's important, one that you will deal with frequently.

The Price-Earnings Ratio

Last but not least, you will need to understand what the *price-earnings ratio* (PE) is and why it is significant. The PE is simple to calculate, but its significance may be somewhat more difficult to grasp. I actually exposed you to the concept already in Chapter 2 when I used the term *multiple* to talk about the price of a business. You should know now why that price is expressed as the number of times a company's income one might be willing to pay for that business.

Perhaps the simplest analogy would be to consider it as a "rate" or "unit price." Very similar to the price you pay for a pound of coffee or a gallon of gas, the PE is the price you pay for a dollar's worth of a company's earnings. And, in the same way that you can tell from experience whether the price of coffee or gasoline is high or low, you can do the same with the price paid for those earnings.

Whether you are evaluating a business as a potential proprietor or as a shareholder, the principle is the same and the notion of expressing the company's value as a multiple of earnings is the same. However, you're buying just a limited number of shares, not the entire business. Therefore, your multiple is expressed in terms of a single share.

The price-earnings ratio (PE, or multiple) is calculated by dividing the current price of a share of the stock by the earnings per share (EPS). The term is widely used because everyone acknowledges that over the long term the price of a stock is tied directly to the company's earnings— even if most short-term players disregard that reality.

For you as a long-term, technamental investor, the PE is the all-important relationship that you will need to explore in order to evaluate the price of a stock. To tie a will-o'-the-wisp figure, such as a stock's price to a solid number such as a company's earnings, is akin to trying to anchor a cloud to a rock! Let's look at the many faces of the PE to get the idea of it.

A Measure of Confidence

The price-earnings ratio is a measure of investor confidence in a company. What brings about that confidence is, of course, the company's ability to add value and make money, thus producing earnings. The more capable of producing earnings a company is—or appears to investors to be—the greater the amount of confidence investors will have and the more they will pay for the stock. And this leads to another facet of the PE.

A Measure of Time

As I said earlier, earnings growth raises the price investors are willing to pay because they will be able to recover their investment in a shorter period of time. With no growth, the PE would actually represent the number of years it would take to recover one's investment. If the company earned $1 per share and the stock sold at a PE of 5, it would take five years at $1 each year to accumulate and recover the money paid for the stock. Who's going to wait that long to get their money back? We might be willing to wait for three years if the company were good and solid. So for a company that's not growing, perhaps a PE of 3 might be reasonable.

Let's say, on the other hand, that a company earning $1 per share were to grow each year at 15 percent compounded. In those three years, we would be able to accumulate not $3 but $4 in earnings. We could therefore justify paying four times earnings (a PE of 4) because we wouldn't have to wait 4 years to make the $4. So in a sense, the PE is a way to look at time.

	Earned	**Accumulation**
First year	$1.15	$1.15
Second year	1.32	2.47
Third year	1.52	3.99

Time is money—or so they say. So it comes down to the fact that the PE is really another way we have to measure how much the stock is worth to us.

A Measure of Value

Veronica Lake, a movie star of my era, had a signature hairdo. One lock of her beautiful blond hair cascaded smoothly down over one eye and then joined the rest of her shoulder-length, neatly coifed tresses. Everyone knew her by her hair.

Golf pros have their signature clubs, and other athletes have their signature equipment, clothing, or even mannerisms. A signature is a particular trait or physical characteristic that is tied to an individual.

So it seems to be with a company and its price-earnings ratio. A company's ability to earn, or to grow its earnings, can be tied to its *fair market value*, the price at which you will find a willing buyer and a willing seller.

This *signature multiple* of earnings will be of interest to us when we evaluate the price of a stock.

A Forecasting Tool

Most writers of traditional investment books won't let you read more than a few chapters before making some reference to the fact that the stock market can be likened to the sea. This is a great metaphor, but most authors just don't carry it nearly far enough.

The stock market is indeed similar to the ocean because, just as a cork floating upon its surface is, the price of a stock is affected by many different influences at once. And each of those forces can either add to or subtract from the effects of the others.

The broadest influence is, of course, the tide that ebbs and flows regularly and in some places rises 50 feet or more above its low point.

Upon the tide are the broad, rolling waves caused by the various disturbances at the sea bottom. Then there are the large waves caused by storms and major changes in the atmosphere, and there are the various ripples and patterns caused by the whim of the local breeze that blows this way and that over a few square yards of the surface.

That cork is buoyed by a combination of all of these influences, some rising and some falling, all at the same time. If you were to try to predict where that cork would be in relation to sea level in the next moment, you'd have a tough time of it. You can't predict what a storm or even an underground earthquake will do to the cork at any given moment. And if you add to that the effects of the winds and the little breezes, it's hopeless!

However, you would be able to forecast, in general, where your cork would bob over the course of a day, instead of at a particular moment. This is because the tides are influenced by the position of the moon, by gravity, and by a variety of other factors that are all scientifically predictable—so predictable, in fact, that almanacs are published that forecast the tides for years ahead, right to the minute.

The stock market is also governed by a diverse set of influences. And just as the sea is, it is predictable over the long term but not over the short term.

Probably the most widely watched reason for the long-term fluctuations of the price and PE is the rise and fall of the stock market itself. This can be a function of the economy's volatility. The economy is battered by the rise and fall of interest rates, by inflation, and by a variety of factors that drive consumer confidence or buying power up or down. Actual changes in the economy itself will cause longer-term changes in the market and the prices of its individual stocks. Speculation about such changes has a shorter-term effect.

In the shorter term, there are the ripples and wavelets. Every little utterance of a government official or company officer, insider buying or selling (which may or may not mean anything), rumor, gossip, and just about anything else can influence the whims of those on the Street. Many people will use these stories to try to make or break a market in the stock.

Over the life of a company, its *signature PE*—the "normal" relationship between a company's earnings and its stock's price—is relatively constant. It does tend to decline slowly as the company's earnings growth declines, which happens with all successful companies. For all practical purposes, however, that relationship is remarkably stable. And for that reason it's also remarkably predictable.

When a company's earnings continue to grow, so will its stock price. Conversely, when earnings flatten or go down, the price will follow.

The little fluctuations in the price-earnings ratio above and below that constant value are not so predictable because they are all caused by investor perception and opinion. Think of them as the winds that blow across the surface of the sea.

The broader moves above and below the norm are the undulations that are typically caused by the continuous rising and falling of analysts' expectations. When a company first emerges into its explosive growth period, the analysts expect earnings to continue to skyrocket. Earnings growth estimates in the 50 percent range or more are not uncommon.

As the company continues to meet these expectations, investor confidence booms along with it, and more investors pay a higher and higher price for the stock. The PE rises as a meteor right along with the price. The faster the growth, the higher the PE. This does nothing to alter the value of the "reasonable" PE multiple. It just means that investor confidence has risen well above that norm and that there will eventually be an adjustment.

Sure enough, one fine day when the analysts' consensus called for growth of 45 percent, the company turns in a "disappointing" earnings growth of only 38 percent. The analysts start wringing their hands because the company has not met their expectations, and some fund manager sells. Next, all of the lemmings on Wall Street follow suit. And not long thereafter you get a call from your broker telling you that you've had a nice ride, you've made a lot of money on the stock, and it's time to take your profit and get out. In the meantime, the broker has made a commission on your purchase and is hoping to make it on your sale as well.

After a while, after the price and the PE have plummeted and then sat there for a while, some analyst wakes up to the fact that a 34 percent earnings growth rate is still pretty darn good and jumps back in. Soon the cycle is reversed. The market starts showing the company some respect again. And you get a call from your broker.

Of course, as a smart technamental investor you didn't sell it in the first place! Because you were watching the fine earnings growth all along, you knew better than to sell. And you chose the opportunity to buy some more. In the meantime, your brokers' clients who were not so savvy had taken their profits (and had paid the taxes on them, by the way) and are now wishing that they had stayed in with you. By the time their broker called them again, the price had already climbed past the point where it made good sense for them to jump in again.

It's best to assume that any price—and therefore PE—movement that is not related to the company's earnings is transient. If the stories—not the numbers—cause the price to move, the change won't last. What goes up will come down, and what goes down will come up. You have to be concerned only when the sales, pretax profits, or earnings cause the change, and then only if you find that the performance decay is related to a major, long-term problem that is beyond management's ability to resolve.

Remember also that a sizable segment of Wall Street doesn't make its money on the ocean as you do; it makes its money on the "ocean motion." Buy or sell, it makes little difference to them what you do. They make their money either way. But it sure makes a big difference to you!

These 10 items—share of stock, sales, assets, expenses, liabilities, profit, equity, earnings per share, book value per share, and price-earnings ratio—represent all the terms you need to know to be able to understand a company. Let's talk about the things you don't need to know.

The "Other 20 Percent"

Within the ranks of NAIC investors, the lore holds that you can learn 80 percent of all you need to know about a company from the Stock Selection

Guide (SSG)—NAIC's printed worksheet. Some—I am among them—would put an even higher percentage on the value of that form or the Technamental Stock Study Worksheet (TSSW), from which most of the illustrations in subsequent chapters have been taken.

What this implies is that, whether it's 20 percent or less, there might be some other things that are important to know. Certainly your confidence will grow as your experience grows and you learn more beyond the basics. These are things you will pick up as your curiosity leads you to learn about them—commonsense things about the companies, their industries, and about business and economics in general. But you don't *need* to know these things to be successful. And, if you're diligent and conservative in working with that 80 or 90 percent you can get from the basics, you will do as well as the average professionals or better.

Of course there's nothing at all wrong with wanting to learn more and more. You should recognize, however, there is a wide and deep chasm between the little you need to know to be successful and the level of learning that puts you in the next echelon above. And, until you have bridged that chasm, the information you pick up as you cross through it is not terribly useful and probably most closely resembles the "little knowledge" that has such a poor reputation for being dangerous. Just be sure you learn enough to keep those things from influencing decisions foolishly.

Your focus would be on *vulnerability*. You are obviously less interested in trying to justify a purchase if it's marginal than in trying to find the flaws that might make an apparently good company not so good, both before and after you purchase its stock. In this respect, there are two aspects to consider: *financial vulnerability* and *operational vulnerability*.

The former deals with the management of things such as debt, leverage, and capitalization. The latter deals with such things as production control, inventory management, collections, and the like. So let's look at these broad topics for a moment and see why doing so passes beyond the point of diminishing returns with respect to your time and energy.

Financial Vulnerability

The three main areas of concern here are *liquidity, leverage*, and *debt service*.

The initial shareholders' investment in the company provides the funds for the purchase of those assets that begin to bring in revenue. Once the operation is profitable enough to ensure that all expenses can be paid comfortably out of revenues, growth is generated by continually plowing profits back into the company to add more assets to generate still more revenue. This is the growth cycle, and the goal is to keep this cycle in motion as long as growth is possible.

Liquidity is the degree to which ready cash is available when needed. It's management's responsibility to have enough cash on hand—to keep the company sufficiently liquid—to meet the payments when due or to handle emergencies when they arise. Plowing the profits back into the company must not be done at the expense of sacrificing sufficient liquidity.

Leverage is the use of other people's money to make money.

Management has the responsibility for wringing the most revenue out of the company's assets. Although a growing company can accelerate its growth by issuing more shares and raising additional funds, the shareholders—the owners—don't want to always have to share the benefits of growth with an increasing number of shareholders. They want their share of the profits to increase for each share they hold.

Debt, therefore, is another source of capital to increase assets. By borrowing money to add to the machines and other things that produce revenue or keep down costs, the additional profit, after the payments on that debt are made, does not have to be shared with any more shareholders. So management has an incentive to increase shareholder value by borrowing. The ability to increase the return on your investment by borrowing to add assets is called *leverage*.

Debt service deals with the capacity of the company to handle its debt. If a company earns enough profit over and above expense, retains enough to remain comfortably liquid so that payments are made in timely fashion, and has sufficient reserves to handle those payments when times are bad and revenues suffer, then management is doing its job.

You will find the definitions of some specific, frequently used ratios and metrics dealing with financial vulnerability in Appendix A along with their calculation and significance.

Why don't you need to worry about any of the "financial vulnerability" items?

1. The **lenders** are your first line of defense, carefully analyzing the wisdom of granting the loans, making those decisions conservatively—without being able to realize the additional benefits of a successful operation, staying on top of the company's continuing ability to make the payments, and having the benefit of more complete and proprietary data than either the shareholders or analysts have access to.

2. **Management** is the second line of defense, carefully treading the fine line between leverage and vulnerability, having to focus on only a single company, monitoring the financial welfare of the company on a daily basis, and also being privy to more proprietary data and corporate insights than you can ever expect to have.

3. **You** can't do anything about it anyway except to sell your stock.

Operational Vulnerability

This refers to the pitfalls that can befall a company when management is not "minding the store" as diligently as it should or when unforeseen problems creep up on them and they make poor decisions to cope with them.

Are there any ways for us to foresee problems cropping up in the way our companies are run before the results hit the street and we suffer along with the crowd? Are there any indicators that we investors might call upon to at least ring an alarm bell if a company is beginning to become operationally vulnerable?

Looking at the tools management uses to operate, we find that most fall into two categories: ratios developed from the income statement and ratios that compare income statement items with significant balance sheet items. Most of these are analyzed over time and compared from one period to the next to look for trends or anomalies.

In the case of the former, management finds it useful to calculate the ratio of just about every item of **expense and income to net sales or revenue**. Rather than list them all, you can just run through the possibilities

67

in your mind and consider them. For example, it's useful to see what percent of sales was contributed by each of the different product lines; or to analyze and compare what percentage of sales was used to pay for raw materials, labor, or transportation. These are supposed to stay within certain reasonable values, and any significant change alerts management to find out the cause and do something about it.

Of those income statement items, the bottom line is the bottom line. The most important by far is the relationship of profit to revenue—or profit margins. And, guess what! We do make that a crucial test of management's efficiency and the company's quality, as you will see in Chapter 9.

Other ratios involve specific balance sheet items. And these are usually compared with either sales or profits. When compared with sales, the ratios are usually expressed as "**turnover**"; when compared with profits, they're usually expressed as "**return**." Thus, asset turnover is the ratio of sales to assets; return on assets is the ratio of profit to the company's assets.

Again, you will find a selection of such metrics in Appendix A along with their definitions and significance.

Why don't you have to worry about any of the "operational vulnerability" items?

1. Management is hired to make the right decisions and to be skilled at using the tools you are curious about, has access to far more data and much sooner than you can access it, and has more at stake than you in doing it right.

2. Professional analysts are "spring-loaded" to jump if anything looks suspicious. Even though you now (thanks to the full-disclosure laws recently enacted) have access to all of the data to which they are privy, without having the time that these defensive players have to devote to watching over out companies, you don't stand a chance of beating them to the punch and spotting these problems far enough ahead to do you any good. They are the "fastest guns in the west" that you'll never be. The very best you might hope for is to pursue your defensive strategy, which you'll find discussed in Chapter 12, and sell those stocks before the majority of the rest of the herd has a chance to react.

The final reason you don't have to worry about these things is the old familiar "Rule of Five," which predicts that one out of every five stocks you buy will disappoint you. Whether it's because unpredictable events such as the death of key management people, the discovery that the company was "cookin' the books," or simply being blindsided by unexpected competition or product obsolescence, these things will happen and you can do nothing to predict those occurrences. Trying to foresee these kinds of things will take much more of your time than it's worth. As happened with the Enron and Worldcom scandals, even the professionals were taken by surprise. So, understanding the Rule of Five will keep you from wasting your time and emotional well-being and kicking yourself in the fanny for missing that one out of five.

Let's Take Stock of   The Terms You Need to Know to Move Ahead

There are only 10 terms you really must know. These terms describe the data that you will use to study your candidates.

1. **Share of stock**—Evidence of your ownership of a part of a company.

Eight terms to measure the company's performance and condition:

Performance (Income Statement)	*Condition (Balance Sheet)*
2. **Sales**— What it takes in ("good")	3. **Assets**—What it owns ("good")
Minus	Minus
4. **Expenses**—What it spends ("bad")	5. **Liabilities**—What it owes ("bad")
Equals	Equals
6. **Profit**—What's left ("good") Divided by shares outstanding	7. **Equity**—What's left ("good") Divided by shares outstanding
8. **Earnings per share**— Your portion	9. **Book value per share**— Your portion

And finally:

10. **Price-earnings ratio (PE, multiple)**—The relationship between the company's earnings and the price of its stock.

From these data you (or your computer) can easily calculate the additional values that you will use to decide whether a company is a good one to invest in and whether its stock is selling for a fair price. You'll learn later where and how you can obtain these data at minimum cost.

Finally, you learned that, though it may be interesting and even entertaining to indulge your curiosity and learn all you can about management's tools of the trade, it's not time well spent to try to employ them to out-guess or second-guess management. There are others out there who, watching out for their own interests, serve to protect you. And, they are effective 80 percent of the time. You can minimize the damage the rest of the time by the simple tasks you will learn later.

If you have not already installed the CD at the back of the book in your computer, and you have a computer available, now is the time to do it. Not only are there quizzes for each of the chapters to test yourself on what you learned, but there is also a section called "Dealing with Data" that will help you solidify in your mind what we have just covered.

Next, we'll talk about the heartbeat of technamental investing: growth.

CHAPTER 5

Understanding Growth

Growth can be defined as an increase in whatever data you're looking at over a period of time. When you study a company, you're looking for the results of management at work—an increase in sales and earnings, quarter after quarter, year after year. This is the basis for your confidence in a company and its ability to grow and make money for you. Remember: Your investment performance is directly related to the company's ability to generate a consistent increase in its earnings.

Sales Growth

Although it's the growth of earnings that promises to double the value of your stock, earnings can't grow without sales growth. It's the growth of sales, after expenses have been deducted, that generates the profit. And it's the profit, divided among the outstanding shares, that produces the earnings. So without sales growth there can be no growth in earnings to increase the value of your stock—at least over the long term.

There are only a few ways sales can grow. And the quality of growth varies with those sources. Let's go back to Lucy's Lemonade Stand so this will be easy to understand.

In order for her sales to grow Lucy has to sell more lemonade each week. To do this she can sell more lemonade to her regular customers, increase the number of customers she sells lemonade to, add cookies or some other products, or pursue a combination of those options. She can also make more money from each customer by raising her prices.

To increase the number of customers she can put flyers in neighborhood mailboxes. She can pay her playmate Charlene to open another stand on the next block. If this puts her in competition with Peter, two blocks away, and she takes some of his customers, she might even be willing to take over Peter's stand for a share of the profits because he's decided he'd rather play baseball.

Adding new products makes sense because she already has the stand, the location, and the customer base. They like her lemonade and will probably try her cookies. And she can experiment with additional products—limeade, raspberry coolers, or whatever—to see whether it makes sense to offer them. Or she can raise prices—but only if she has no competition and if her customers will support it.

There's little or no difference between this and what a big company does to grow, but what management must do to accomplish these things is a bit more complicated.

Probably the healthiest growth in revenues is referred to as *organic growth*—growth that is generated by either marketing or research and development.

Successful marketing will add new users for the product from among those who have never used such a product before, or it will take customers (market share) away from competitors that sell a similar product. This activity might include creating new markets geographically—abroad, perhaps. Or the company might expand its customer base demographically—maybe marketing a product to older or younger users than were targeted before.

Research and development will add more products or services to put in the marketplace. Hopefully these will be related to the company's existing products or services and will not be outside of the company's customary business domain.

Peter Lynch calls such unrelated expansion "deworsification." It wouldn't be smart for Lucy to offer pet food when her success is based upon her gustatory delights for the *human* palate.

Also effective, but perhaps less healthy, is the *acquisition* of other companies. A strong company gobbles up the weaker ones in the same or similar businesses. Where allowed by the government, it eliminates competition, adds the acquired companies' sales to the top line, and hopefully finds some economies of scale and some synergies that will benefit the bottom line as well.

What makes acquisition riskier than organic growth is that the acquiring company will likely inherit not only the acquired company's assets and additional business but also the problems that made the company weak enough to grab. Labor problems can be easy to turn around, given an enlightened corporate culture and the eagerness of the labor force to cooperate with new and benevolent management. But plant and equipment obsolescence, bad brand reputation, or other more deep-rooted, long-term problems can be harder to overcome.

Another means of growing the top line is to raise prices. This is a very risky step that works only in certain situations. Generally, competition limits those possibilities and, even if there's virtually no competition, the price doesn't usually go up without some decline in the units sold, There are some cases, though, where price increases add substantially to a company's revenues without a sacrifice at the bottom line. For example, consider a drug company that enjoys the protection of a patent for each new product as it emerges from its pipeline. It can take advantage of that unique protection from competition and push prices up with little fear of decline in units sold.

When you look at a company and consider it for investment, it's a good idea to ask yourself where the company's growth comes from. Is the growth organic? Or is it coming from acquisitions? Is the company adding products or invading new markets? How aggressive is the company's international business, or is there a potential to expand there? What, if any, are the company's barriers to competition (sometimes referred to as its "moat")? If you can't answer these questions at first, don't worry! You'll learn as you go along. And as you will soon discover, you can do an excellent job of picking your stocks without going into detail about such things. You should know something about the product and its market, though, if only on a basic consumer's level. Commonsense issues can and should influence you when it comes to feeling at home with your candidates.

Earnings Growth

Where can earnings growth come from? Let's look at Lucy's Lemonade Stand again.

Lucy has taken over Peter's stand. Charlene runs another stand next to the playground. Lucy financed this growth primarily from profits, but also by hitting up Uncle Harry for 30 bucks in return for a piece of the action. "By now," Lucy's dad had told Harry, "she's up to about $50 a week and her business is growing pretty fast."

To be sure, earnings should be growing as fast as sales because it's her sales that produce the profit—after taking into account the cost of lemons and sugar and the 50 cents an hour she pays Charlene and little Douglas, who runs Peter's old stand.

Aside from the volume of sales—the source of earnings and the basic generator of growth—why might earnings grow any faster or slower? We'll look at that issue in greater detail in Chapter 13. For now I'll just cover the high points.

There are only two other factors that will affect earnings: expenses and outstanding shares. We'll consider expenses first because they're easier to understand.

Lucy's lemon cost can rise or fall. It can rise because the cost of lemons at the store rises (a bad season in California) or because she has to pay someone to go to the market to get them. Her lemon cost can fall because the store's produce manager gives her a special volume price.

Lucy's labor cost can rise. Charlene had been working for a quarter an hour, but someone put a bug in her ear and told her she should be getting three times as much. She demanded 75 cents, but Lucy talked her friend back down to a half dollar.

Lucy has now started making enough money that her dad's going to have to show her income on his tax return. She's going to have to start saving up to reimburse Dad for the taxes. So she figures out the profits each week and puts aside a percentage of that to give her dad the following April.

Uncle Harry's share is just like common stock: He simply put money into the business, never expecting Lucy to pay it back. But he is entitled to a third of the profits.

If Uncle Harry had simply lent her the $30 with the expectation that she would pay him back in a year, it would have been a loan, and Lucy's expenses would have included paying him interest on that loan. Harry would then have held a bond rather than a share of stock. The downside to Lucy would have been the requirement that she pay Uncle Harry even when a spell of rainy weather kept the stand closed. The upside would be that she would owe Uncle Harry no more in good times than in bad. All of the extra money she might make from the money Uncle Harry lent to her would belong to her and her father—her original stockholder. Again, this is *leverage*: making money by using OPM (other people's money).

Lucy might have worked out yet another deal with Uncle Harry for the 30 bucks. He could have given her the money with no requirement that she pay him back. There would be two conditions, though. She would have to agree to pay him a fixed *dividend* every month as long as she stayed in business. And if the lemonade business folded, Uncle Harry would have first crack at whatever could be salvaged to recover his investment—even before her dad would. But as her profits rose, her payments to Uncle Harry wouldn't. This is the nature of *preferred stock*. Even though these *preferred dividends* represent a distribution to a shareholder, they are considered an expense, much as interest is, and they would be paid before Lucy or her dad or any other common stockholders would be entitled to their shares.

But as it is, Lucy now has to split the take not only with her dad, but also with Uncle Harry. So whereas every dollar's worth of profit meant 50 cents each to Lucy and her dad before Uncle Harry came along, it now represents a little more than 33 cents. But thanks to Uncle Harry, the business is now bringing in many more dollars of profit than it would have without his participation, so she's happy to split the profit with Uncle Harry, too.

Any of these things can cause the earnings per share to grow at a faster or slower rate than sales. And all of them simply require common sense to understand. Let's apply them to a large company.

As we said, earnings growth is first a function of sales growth. Earnings, *over the long term*, can grow no faster than sales. Remember that, when you look at a company, it's a good idea to understand where that sales growth comes from.

Earnings growth is a function of one of three things: sales growth, expenses, and shares outstanding. (Although tax is an expense as any other, it's dependent upon profits. When you evaluate growth, you'll find it of more significance to consider the profits before taxes have been paid. This will let you look more closely at how management handles the things over which it has some control.)

Expenses

As with Lucy's Lemonade Stand, for a large company variable and fixed expenses can fluctuate up or down for many reasons. Material costs can increase, the cost of labor can rise—all are expenses related to producing the product or service.

In addition, there are fixed expenses, things such as rent, interest on bonds, insurance, management's salaries, equipment leases, and the cost of replacing equipment that has become obsolete or worn (*depreciation*). As would have been the case with Lucy if she had borrowed the money from Uncle Harry, fixed expenses have to be paid no matter how good or bad business is.

All of these expenses affect the bottom line. The *profit margin* is simply the percentage of sales that remains after all of these expenses have been paid. It represents the number of pennies out of every dollar of sales the company gets to keep to either plow back into the company (retain to equity) or pay out in dividends to the shareholders.

Shares Outstanding

Earnings per share—your portion of the company's profits—are what drive the value of your investment. So, in addition to considering an increase or decline in the profit margin, you must look for earnings growth or decline based on the number of shares among which the profits are divided.

Before Uncle Harry got involved, Lucy had only her father to share the profits with. Now she and her dad have to share them with Uncle Harry, the new shareholder. This is called *dilution*, because the amount of profit going to each shareholder is diluted when it must be split among additional shares.

If a company sells additional shares, the existing shareholders will see an increase in the equity of the company as the money paid for the stock goes in the bank. But the book value per share will not change very much if at all because the number of shares has increased, diluting the value of that equity for each share. And when the income statement comes out at the end of the period, they will find that the earnings per share (EPS) will have declined from what it might have been had the shares not been issued.

The issuing of *convertible debentures* is another consideration. These are instruments that are purchased as bonds—the money is lent to the company—but that may, at a later date and at the discretion of the holder, be turned in for common stock. There is a potential for greater dilution here. When someone decides to exercise the conversion option, the company's obligation to repay the loan will be over, so it will be the same as if the stockholder had purchased the stock earlier. The money is in the bank. Again, however, the number of shares among which the profit must be allocated will have grown to whatever extent those bonds have been converted.

Another source of dilution, especially with new, high-tech companies, has been the practice of issuing stock options as compensation. To be competitive in the labor market, more and more companies have had to offer employees an opportunity to cash in at a later date on the company's growth. However, in recent times, there has been a movement for companies to show these stock options as an expense to the company. This, plus the desire of employees to enjoy the security of a regular paycheck in the aftermath of all the company failures early in the 2000s, has substantially reduced the incentives to follow that practice.

Earnings must be reported both as *basic* and as *diluted* earnings. You're interested in the diluted earnings—as are most analysts—because they reflect the result of distributing earnings among all possible shares. This offers the worst-case view of earnings and represents the most conservative approach to assessing the company's performance.

Many times earnings will show growth despite the fact that neither sales nor profit margins have grown. In fact, either or both may have declined. When this happens, there is only one explanation: share repurchase. If a company has repurchased its shares, the opposite of dilution takes place as the company's profits are distributed among fewer shares. You'll find out later how to tell at a glance when share repurchase has caused earnings to grow without accompanying sales growth.

You will also learn later how to diagnose at a glance the reasons that earnings and sales are growing at different rates. For the time being, suffice it to say that any difference in the rates of growth can't last forever. The two must settle into a state of equilibrium eventually, or the company will go out of business. If earnings grow faster than sales, the cutting of costs or the buying back of shares cannot go on forever. If earnings grow at a slower rate than sales, the company will die if management isn't capable of stanching the outflow of money in expenses. And, of course, there's a limit to how much stock a company can issue when earnings per share are declining.

Let's Take Stock of	What You Need to Know About Growth

➤ The value of a stock is measured by the multiple of earnings (PE) that investors are willing to pay for it.

➤ The value of your investment grows when the company's earnings grow at a rate that increases the value of the stock at approximately the same rate.

➤ The rate of earnings growth depends upon the rate of sales growth but can, for a limited period, vary above or below it.

➤ Earnings per share are affected by expenses and by changes in the number of shares outstanding.

➤ You are interested in finding companies that are capable of producing earnings growth sufficient to double your investment about every five years.

With this understanding of growth under your belt, let's go on to learn about how to identify the companies that can deliver the growth for you're seeking.

CHAPTER 6

Prospecting for Good Candidates

Some Sound Principles

NAIC teaches its members four principles that have become something of a mantra. They represent excellent advice and are worthy of mention here:

1. *Invest a fixed amount regularly*. Successful investing requires discipline. This principle is especially important for young folks who have the opportunity to put aside a small amount on a regular basis, an amount that can add up over the years to become a substantial fortune. But it can also apply to clubs that collect dues that are to be invested on a regular basis.

   When you invest a fixed amount regularly, you enjoy the benefits of *dollar cost averaging*: You will buy more shares when they are cheap and fewer when they are expensive. This should provide for a lower cost per share over time.

2. *Reinvest all earnings*. This is sound advice if you are going to maximize your investment benefits. The magic of compounding—earning money on your earned money—is very important. It makes the difference between being able

to double your money every five years or putting that objective beyond reasonable reach. If you pull out your earnings every year instead of reinvesting them, it will take a return of 20 percent a year to double your investment. If you leave your earnings where they are, doubling your investment will take but 15 percent per year. The former is beyond reasonable reach, the latter an attainable goal.

3. *Invest only in good-quality growth companies*. As I've said over and over, growth is what drives the price of stocks. You will want to find those companies that, on the average, can double your money every five years.

4. *Diversify*. Without a doubt, it's foolish to put all your eggs in one basket. Having too high a percentage of your portfolio in only one company, a single industry, or a particular size of company can subject you to unnecessary risk. However, this principle is more often given too much emphasis than not enough. (See Chapter 13 for a more detailed discussion.)

Of these four fine principles, the first two and the last are fairly mechanical and depend upon a simple sense of discipline. The third, however, is the most important and is the one that causes the most concern. That is why I have devoted most of this book to that topic.

One additional principle that is appropriate to mention here is: *If it looks too good to be true, it probably is*. This is one thing that many people find out from their own experiences, unfortunately. When you learn how to analyze and evaluate a company, you'll occasionally find a stock that appears to be a bargain. It rarely is. You'll be wise to be skeptical and suspicious—curious to find out why the price is so low rather than eager to make a killing.

Keep your expectations and ambitions modest and reasonable. You'll earn your success by seeking a win-win situation that results from adding value that someone else will be only too pleased to pay for. Once in a while you may be able to take advantage of a situation in which a stock is seriously undervalued by investors, but most of the time you'll find that you're prospecting among fairly valued stocks. That's where you will find most of your winners.

You can accomplish your goal of doubling your money in five years by investing in a business, because earnings growth of 15 percent is a reasonable goal for a well-run business. When you look to do very much better than that, you're straying into territory in which someone else has to lose for you to gain. This is the "BFS/STS" scenario that grossly decreases your odds for success.

There are more than 10,000 publicly owned companies out there for you to select from. And those are just the ones in the United States. Some are, of course, much better candidates for your consideration than others. Of these 10,000 companies, fewer than 2 percent are likely to make the cut so far as your quality standards are concerned. And perhaps only 5 percent of *those* might be available at the right price at any given time—and even this could be an overestimate.

How About a Mutual Fund?

"Aha!" you say. Based on those four principles that are important enough to commit to memory, it sounds as though a mutual fund would be the perfect choice. Let's see:

The first principle says to invest a fixed amount regularly.

Check. That's what you do with a mutual fund. You commit to sending in a fixed amount every month. The discipline is taken care of and so is the dollar cost averaging. Perfect!

Reinvest all income.

Check. That's what they do. Your dividends remain in the account and are added to the value of the fund. Great!

Invest only in good-quality growth companies.

Check again. Not only can I select a fund that announces its intention to do just that but I can look at its track record to see how well it's done.

Diversify.

Perfect! A fund isn't limited to only as many stocks as I can keep track of in my spare time. It can own 1,000 stocks or 10,000 stocks and has a professional staff watching over them all day, every day.

What could be a more perfect way to apply the four principles?

Not so fast! True, investing in mutual funds offers the opportunity to do exactly what I've built a case for thus far: owning small pieces of growing concerns. And it's certainly much better than putting your money under your mattress or in a tin can buried in your backyard. If you pick the right fund, you should be able to do better than you would with a CD or a money market account, or with bonds.

I've made the point that your aim is to minimize your risks and responsibilities while still getting the best possible return from owning parts of a business or businesses. I've led you down the road from starting your own business to owning shares of stock in a number of companies, and I've explained that you have to pay increasing multiples of earnings as you shed responsibilities and risks.

Mutual funds, however, are overkill. They carry you past the point where you can get the most return for the least cost.

Investing in a good mutual fund is a temporary alternative that you should pursue only long enough to develop confidence and skill in this simple and effective approach. It's a good way to build your beginning nest egg. However, I think you'll be paying more than you should for the privilege of relieving yourself of further responsibility and risk. Here's why.

First of all, the premise that you can satisfy the most important principle by simply selecting the fund that has the appropriate objective and the best track record is not the "no-brainer" it sounds like. The government rigidly regulates funds—what they report and how they report—so you can find out about their track records if you know where to look and what to look for. Or you can seek the help of a professional who does. However, the government can't dictate what a fund chooses to advertise as long as it's accurate. Naturally, a fund will put its best foot forward, and if you rely on anything less rigorous than the prospectus, you will have a hard time comparing "apples to apples." There are, however, fine services such as Morningstar (*www.morningstar.com*) that have done a creditable job of standardizing the way performance is calculated and presented. But, it's often hard for the novice to tell how each fund's record is figured from what they usually have to go on.

Let's say, though, that you could standardize performance figures and could look at several funds side by side, comparing them on that basis. What do you have to go on that assures you that their future performance will be anything like their history? Without being able to look at each stock in the fund's portfolio and to analyze it yourself (I suppose you could, but I think you'd rather have a life), you can't really assess the future.

More important, there's nothing that says that those same stocks will be there next week. When I talk about a "track record," it's truly apropos in this context, because trying to assess the future performance of a mutual fund can be likened to trying to handicap a horse race by looking at the jockey's record. With a mutual fund you're looking at the record of the "jockey" that manages the fund. Jockeys change horses and fund managers move around, too. There's nothing to assure you that the same manager will continue to manage your fund or that his success will necessarily continue if he stays on. You're betting your money on the jockey and not on the horse!

For that privilege you're likely to pay a commission either on the money you pay at the start (*front-end load*) or an even a bigger amount on the higher value that the fund should be worth at a later time (*back-end load*). There are also no-load funds for which no commissions are paid. But don't kid yourself! Someone has to pay everyone who manages the fund, sells it, promotes it, and does all of the paperwork. And after covering the cost of that infrastructure, the mutual fund company has to make a profit for its stockholders just as any other company does. So you'll always find a management fee amounting to some percentage of your investment buried somewhere in the contract.

Having more than 15 or 20 good companies in your portfolio isn't going to be all that productive for you anyway. You don't need more companies to minimize your risk, and there are not all that many above-average companies out there. The more companies you own beyond a certain point, the more mediocre your portfolio's performance is likely to be. Warren Buffett, one of the most successful investors of all time, has only about a dozen major positions—not 30 companies in all—in his portfolio. Who are we to argue?

On top of that, because fund managers are handling other people's money and not just their own, there are many things you can do that they can't. You can take advantage of some opportunities that fund managers

85

can't or won't. You can buy or sell all the shares of a stock without having to worry about whether your transaction will affect the price of the stock, whereas large-fund managers have to worry about how selling their positions will affect the market for that stock because they control so much of it.

For me, however, the most compelling argument is this: Although one fund may have a slower turnover rate for its holdings than others, its manager cannot sit still and wait out a bump in the road the way you can. Those stocks are bought and sold all the time, and the fund managers have to churn those accounts to capture profits and show off the portfolio every quarter. Every time they do it, they incur a tax liability that you have to pay, and at the end of the year you'll feel it.

So I suggest that you park your money in mutuals only long enough to earn some money while you find the stocks you want to buy individually. Once you've assembled your own portfolio, you can start paying *yourself* all of the money you'll save.

Before leaving this topic, I should mention one new brokerage concept that can provide all of the benefits of mutual fund investing with practically none of the drawbacks mentioned in this section. This is called *folio investing*. A good source of information concerning this concept is *The Folio Phenomenon* by Gene Walden (Dearborn Trade, 2002). Essentially, these brokerages do "window trading," which means that they consolidate all of their clients' orders into a single trade and go to the market only at specified times, which may range from as often as twice a day to as few as once a week, depending on the brokerage. They pass the savings on to their clients in the form of lower commissions, and, of greatest significance, they apportion the holdings to their clients in fractional shares.

This means that you may invest 50 dollars or $10 thousand in as many or as few stocks as you wish at any time. Thus, you can start out with a small amount of money, select the stocks you wish to invest in, and have the brokerages invest whatever percentage of your dollars you may wish in each of those stocks. This is ideal for investing a fixed amount regularly.

As a long-term investor, window trading will not materially affect your performance and can cut your costs of buying and selling. Folio*fn* (*www.foliofn.com*), one of the pioneers in this concept, does its trading twice a day and, as of this writing, charges only four dollars per trade, or $199 a year for unlimited transactions. This is a concept worthy of exploring for your needs and is a very inexpensive and effective way to start investing without the need to have a sizeable nest egg to start your portfolio.

However you decide to do it, your first job in assembling your portfolio will be to separate the wheat from the chaff and to select good prospects to study.

Looking for Candidates

Candidate is certainly an appropriate word here. No candidate serves in office without being put in that office through an appropriate election process. And no candidate should become a part of your portfolio until it passes your stringent selection process. But without some candidates, we have nothing to elect or to select from.

We now know the terms. Let's apply them to our preliminary task of prospecting for good candidates for *study*—not yet for purchase.

What You're Not Looking For

Before I tell you about what you want in a company, let me tell you about the qualities that you *don't* want. That way you'll be able to eliminate a whole lot of companies right off the bat.

Not old enough. Companies that have not been trading publicly long enough to have an audited track record are not good candidates. You don't want to bother with a company that hasn't had at least five years of public trading on one of the major exchanges.

This, of course, rules out initial public offerings (IPOs) and other such speculative situations. If someone suggests such an investment to you, check the financial pages in the newspaper for starters. If the stock doesn't appear in the NYSE, AMEX, or NASDAQ listings, tell your friend, "Thanks for the suggestion, but no thanks!"

Not big enough. Companies that, despite their age, have not grown to at least $50 million in sales are too small to be interesting. In fact, with rare exceptions, you're better off skipping companies that have not yet achieved $100 million in sales. As with landing fish below the limit, you should throw them back in and let them grow some more. Rest assured, you won't miss out on anything.

Put the attractive "minnows" on your watch list when they're small. If they're capable of the kind of growth you think they are, they'll continue to grow until they have earned your confidence. And you'll still be able to get in before the rest of the world finds out enough about them to jump on the bandwagon.

Not earning yet. Companies with no earnings are not a good bet for reasons you should know by now. No matter how sexy a company's story may be, unless it has acquired a solid track record of taking in more than it pays out, it can't last very long any more than you could under the same circumstances.

Wait for the start-ups to start making money—and then wait for them to make it for a while longer. I guarantee you it won't be too late for you to make money with them.

I guess this is as good a time as any to address that dot-com bubble of the 1990s and the subsequent bust. The lessons to be learned from those events are important.

The stock market of the 1990s ought to be looked upon as a special case. It was a modern day, real-live bubble, and many of us hadn't lived through such a thing. The dot-com bubble challenged all that we knew and held dear. And it was an excellent example of what Charles McKay wrote about way back in 1841 in his wonderful book *Extraordinary Delusions and the Madness of Crowds.* If McKay had lived in the 20th century, he would have written with equal clarity and derision about the chain letters of 1935 and the dot-com bubble of the 1990s.

Webster's dictionary offers as a definition of the word *bubble*: "any idea, scheme, etc. that seems plausible at first but quickly shows itself to be worthless or misleading." Generally speaking, an economic bubble develops when, on a large scale, buyers discard the rational assessment of the value of something and award to it a value that is based solely upon what they think someone else might be willing to pay for it.

Merchants and huge discount empires can't afford to mark up their merchandise to a level that exceeds the normal customer's willingness to pay for value received. Competition and availability of the merchandise keep the lid on. The exception, of course, is when the supply of some fad (such as the Pokemon cards, Beanie Babies, or Tomogatchi pets) is limited and the prices become inflated for a while—just long enough for the supply to catch up with the pumped-up demand. But these are occasional events throughout history when the madness of crowds has prevailed.

One of the best-known bubbles of history was the tulip-bulb fiasco back in the mid-1630s. For much the same reason that companies without earnings were sought after in the 90s, tulips became so popular that the price was driven up until tulip bulbs were selling for as much as $100,000 apiece!

The story goes that on one occasion, a sailor, thinking it was an onion, ate a tulip bulb, the value of which was equal to the year's salary for him and all of his shipmates. Of course he landed in jail for many months for his culinary indiscretion—and I don't imagine the bulb tasted that good.

To give you a feel for just how full of hot air the recent modern-day bubble was, Keith Mullins, an emerging growth strategist at Salomon Smith Barney, pointed out in a report dated November 19, 1999, that if an investor had put his money into all of the stocks in the Russell 2000 (an index of small, publicly traded companies) at the beginning of 1999, he would have made 6.6 percent on his money for the year. However, if he had placed his money only in the Russell 2000 companies that *lost* money that year—that had no earnings—he would have made 49.7 percent on his investment! Mullins went on to say that the Russell Midcap Index was even more ridiculous. The gain for the entire index was a meager 8 percent, whereas investment in only the losers would have made you 107 percent!

What caused the bubble? One could offer a potpourri of reasons. For starters: the presence of a lot of money that needed to go to work somewhere; economic euphoria; confidence in an economy driven largely by technological initiatives, many of which are paying off. In large measure, the bubble can be attributed to an uneducated public's over-expectation of the impact of the Internet on our lives.

Probably the biggest blast of hot air to pump up this bubble came from the host of young people who made millions in the technology sector early on—who had exercised their stock options and were looking for a way to make millions more with their windfalls.

These new venture capitalists said, "Never mind the earnings. Just get out there and cultivate the mind-share." (*Mind-share* is cyber-speak for the number of eyeballs that come to a Website and hang out there.)

Collectively, the new investors had billions of dollars, and they played only one level above the investors they hoped would jump in when they took their dot-coms public. They were counting on the investing public to take their companies off their hands based on the income potential from those ads.

However, a venture capitalists' bubble can burst, too—and in this case it did, just as soon as they discovered the hard way that *someone* has to earn the money to pay for such things as the exalted salaries, cushy offices, impressive perks, and the other trappings of those unseasoned business managers who were going to lead these fledgling dot-coms from initial capitalization phase to IPO.

Other casualties deriving from the demise of the dot-coms were the huge technology companies such as Intel, Cisco, and others that had committed massive capital infusions to ramping up to serve this exciting new crop of customers for their high-tech wares. As inventories of perishable products overflowed (there's hardly anything more perishable than high-tech equipment, which typically becomes obsolete in 18 months), and sales declined, the fallout was staggering!

Of course, the stock market bubble burst as soon as the investing public decided that it was time to look closer at how much the company earned rather than how plausible or exciting its story seemed to be.

The moral of the story: Don't put your money into any company that doesn't have an established record of earning money for its shareholders, no matter how alluring its story may seem to be.

A secondary but equally important lesson to be learned was that, throughout all of the expansion and sudden collapse of that bubble, good companies were available at the right price. Those investors who were not lured by the apparent easy bucks to be made in the glamour stocks but who stuck by the discipline taught within the covers of this book were rewarded for their patience and discipline.

Not familiar to you. You should reduce your risk further by eliminating from consideration companies that sell products or services that you either don't know about or have no interest in learning about. Peter Lynch often said that he steered clear of technology companies because he knew nothing about what they did. If you don't understand Internet technology, don't get involved with a company that sells routers, no matter how hot a company such as Cisco (CSCO) may appear! There are plenty of other companies that you can nominate as good candidates.

Perhaps this admonition is a little too restrictive. If you're a person who is interested in learning about new things—someone who finds it exciting to devour articles about new technology or whose natural curiosity leads you to find out about things with which you're not familiar, then you should certainly expand your horizons and include companies that are in fields that interest you. It will add to your education and give you an even greater incentive to indulge your intellectual quests. But, unless you do make it a point to educate yourself about the new industry and its idiosyncrasies, you should pay heed to this advice.

Why avoid such a company? It's not because you can't readily determine from its financial statistics that it's potentially a good company to invest in. It's because, once you own its stock, it's harder for you to understand such issues as the market for its products, the risks and potential pitfalls, the significance of new products, or the potential for competition—some of the commonsense factors that may guide your later decision about whether you should sell or hold onto it.

Keep in mind that your intentions are honorable. As a long-term investor, you're going to "marry" this company, not just have an affair with it as the traders do. Just as in real life, the better you understand your mate, the better you'll get along with him or her—or, in this case, it.

What *Are* You Looking For?

This book started with the premise that you should invest in common stocks because they are "live," not "dead" places to put your money. Let's talk for a bit about the "life" of a successful company.

Human beings start life with promise. They look cute and appealing (or red-faced and squalling), but no matter what they're like to begin with, if all goes well, they grow physically, mentally, and emotionally through infancy, childhood, adolescence, and finally adulthood and maturity.

They start by being demanding and dependent. Along the way, they learn how to cope with life, how to be independent. And—again, if all goes well—they learn a set of skills; they learn how to contribute and how to get the most out of life by making that contribution. They also, hopefully, learn a set of values that makes life worthwhile.

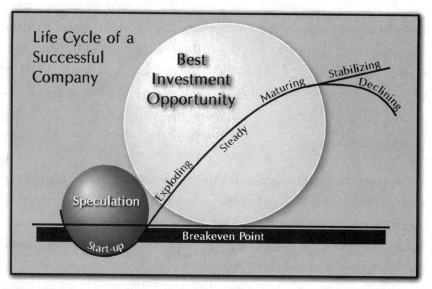

Figure 6.1. Life Cycle of a Successful Company

Some of life's phases are painful, some are awkward, and many are exciting, and eventually in the mature years things simmer down some. Then folks seem to either capitalize on their experience and their resources to make life continually interesting or, at the other extreme, they sink into maudlin reminiscence and dependency.

One could easily compare the stages in the life cycle of a successful business to all of these human phases of growth.

A company at start-up is certainly demanding and dependent. It requires an infusion of capital and sweat equity from risk-takers. And as you can see in Figure 6.1, its earnings are predictably below the breakeven point.

It takes a while before the company can begin to stand on its own two feet and be productive. The process that most companies go through as individual ownership gives way to public ownership and professional management is often painful—akin to the worst kind of growing pains and adolescent turmoil.

Eventually the company breaks even, then learns to focus on what it does best. It begins to fine-tune its operations, to get focused, and to become solidly productive. It generates steady profits; develops a customer base, brand satisfaction, and loyalty; and achieves sufficient credibility to sell its stock to the public.

At the beginning of this explosive growth period, the percent increase in sales and earnings can be spectacular. Obviously, it's easy to grow 100 percent in a year if sales and earnings were inconsequential to begin with. If a company sells $1,000 of goods or services in the first year, it's easy to sell $2,000 the next—much easier than it would be to double sales in the year following a million-dollar year. This phenomenon is referred to as the "law of large numbers." So growth rates early in the life cycle of a successful company tend to be sensational.

The adult years—those years when the physical growth in a human is superseded by mental and emotional growth—correspond to the company's most productive years. These years are characterized by the development of a positive corporate culture (in the best-run companies) and of a corporate ethic and set of values. The results in productivity may not be traced directly to the top or bottom line, but without them success would be impossible. It's the degree to which companies develop in this area that creates "franchise value"—the premium above its peers in its industry at which its stock will consistently sell.

Eventually the successful company reaches a mature growth period when revenue becomes so large that it is difficult to maintain a consistent percentage increase in growth. Just as a human does in the golden years, the company enters a period of stabilization—or it declines if it fails to rejuvenate its product mix or expand its markets.

93

You're interested in finding companies that are at least five years into their explosive growth period—businesses that have completed their adolescence, but have not gone past their prime into decline. Obviously, the longer the company has had a successful track record, the more stable and safe it's apt to be—provided its management copes successfully with maturity.

These are the standards you should stick with when you look for companies to invest in. Higher-risk situations involving companies early in their life cycle are speculative and not of investment quality.

Where Do You Find Investment-Quality Companies?

You can find investment-quality companies everywhere. There are nearly as many good ways to prospect for candidates as there are candidates. Here are just a few.

The Financial Press

Read the financial newspapers. Subscribe to one of the many newsletters that are out there, or just accept the trial offers you will receive when you get on one of their mailing lists. Financial newspapers are full of exciting stories about "wonderful" companies that all try to outdo each other, bragging about their track records. However, none of the newsletters do any better selecting stocks than you can. It's fine to get ideas from them and see what the analysts are saying about some of the comers. But don't buy what the newsletters are selling until you do your own stock study.

Newspapers

Be sensitive to information about industries and specific companies in the regular newspapers. Look for exciting companies. Not only will you find good prospects in the financial pages, but frequently stories about exciting companies will appear in other parts of the paper when something newsworthy affects them. Buried in reports about discoveries or developments in the medical or scientific field will be the names of companies that are working with the new technologies.

The Wall Street Journal (*www.wsj.com*) and *Investors Business Daily* (*www.investors.com*) are both great sources of information about likely prospects.

Television

Some commercials are not worth watching; they just provide you with a good opportunity to go to the refrigerator. But don't be too hasty. You'll find some commercials that are engaging and are marketing enticing products.

Whether you would use the products or not, you might see great value for the market they serve and have an interest in the companies that produce and sell them. As do newspapers, newscasts often have special features that reveal interesting discoveries or developments. With a little research you can dig up companies that are involved in those activities and that might prove to be great investments.

Your Broker

Ask your broker for a suggestion or two. Although I recommend that you *never* take a broker's suggestion and buy a stock without doing your own study, a good, conscientious broker who's interested in your success is an asset to you. Brokers have access to much more research material than you have at your disposal, so it's appropriate that you ask them for the information you want.

If your broker tries to "sell" you on buying an issue, be nice but firm and say that you want the research, not the advice. Ask the specific questions that you want answers to, but don't ask for the broker's opinion. You'd be surprised how soon your broker starts asking you for advice once you start to build a successful portfolio.

Common sense and a little observation are far better providers of stock tips than the average broker whose company may have its own interests at heart when it "suggests" he push a stock! In fact, only a couple of years before this writing, an investigation of 10 of the nation's top brokerage firms by the Securities and Exchange Commission (SEC) and New York's Attorney General's office resulted in those firms having to pay a settlement of some 1.4 *billion* dollars for engaging in just such an activity.

Many people prefer to use discount or online brokers. They offer some research resources, but they don't give advice and they don't pressure you to buy anything.

Your Barber or Beautician

You can get a good or bad tip from anyone. I once got a tip from a bellman in a hotel in Mexico City. He had overheard it from some visiting dignitaries and passed it along to me. Fortunately, I didn't go right home and buy the stock (I might have, because I didn't know then what I know now). I don't remember what the stock was anymore, but I do remember that it turned out to be a bummer!

The point is, of course, that you can get a tip from anyone at any time, but you should do your homework on the company before you buy its stock.

The Shopping Mall or Grocery Store

Find out the names of the companies that produce the products and services that you use and think are excellent. This is a wonderful way to prospect because it takes into account the quality of the products, and you're familiar with the market and with the potential of the products or services.

Peter Lynch says that one of his greatest stock picks was L'Eggs, the hosiery sold in supermarkets. His wife came home one day enthusing about the notion that shoppers could so conveniently purchase hosiery while they were food shopping. He decided to take a look at the company and did buy it—but only after thoroughly researching it.

Products and services that you have specific knowledge of or experience with fit in here as well. If you're a doctor, you'll be familiar with pharmaceuticals. If you're a secretary, you may have had some good and bad experiences with certain brands of office equipment.

Your Children's Playroom

The fastest-growing market today may be the children's market. Toys, clothes, books—anything and everything that kids might want—are selling like hotcakes. Kids have more influence in the home these days than ever, and parents are buying what their children want. This trend may continue until the next generation comes of age, so you might want to look at companies that provide things kids want.

The moral of this story is simply that you should be alert to the economics of what's around you. The booming children's market may be only a transient phenomenon; parents may have run out of money or patience by the time you read this. You will want to size up the trends of your time and look to your own common sense to decide whether they're just fads or are here to stay. If you identify some long-term trends, look for the companies that will let you profit from them.

The Library

The library is a rich source of candidates to study. Not only are there plenty of magazines and other publications that are full of interesting articles and stories about intriguing companies, but there are also reference books that you can access. Some of these offer you names of companies to look at and the data that you need to study them.

The *Value Line Survey* is such a resource. To subscribe to this service, which is available either as a CD-ROM or in printed form, would cost you more than $500 annually. At the library you can find it for free, most likely in print. Probably the most highly respected source of data that you can access at the library, the *Value Line Survey* contains data for its basic list of around 1,700 companies and provides somewhat less information for an additional 1,800 businesses.

The *Value Line Survey* also provides you with lists of companies that meet certain screening requirements. For example, it lists all of the companies that have earnings growth rates above 13 percent per year and expectations of five more years of growth. It also offers a list of companies that are expected to do well over the next three to five years. We'll go into greater detail about *Value Line* later, when we discuss the various sources of information required for your studies.

For now, suffice it to say that the *Value Line Survey* is a great source of possible candidates for your study, and you can kill two birds with one stone by accessing the data required for your analysis as well.

97

An Investment Club

You can start an investment club or join an existing club. Investment clubs are an excellent source of high-quality candidates, and you have the added benefit of collaborating with others who want to learn as you do. If you belong to a club where everyone is as eager to learn as you are, your learning will accelerate as you go along.

The new *NAIC Official Guide, Introduction to Successful Investing Handbook*, can help you start your own club. This publication is far easier reading than its predecessor and is a big help to those organizing a club. (It may be obtained from NAIC's online store at *store.yahoo.com/betterinvesting/st1020.html*.)

NAIC Events

NAIC events are happening all the time, all across the country. Look for NAIC in your local phone directory or visit NAIC's Website (*www.better-investing.org*) to obtain the name and number of the NAIC representative in your area.

You'll soon be talking to a volunteer who can steer you to the next event where you can form wonderful associations with folks who have embarked on the same path you're setting out on. NAIC not only can help you come up with good candidates for study, but it can help you find a club to join or a workshop to go to that will help you learn more about what you're reading now and offer you more opportunities to network with others with the same interest.

NAIC Online

NAIC's online presence, the so-called I-Club, or online investment club, is an army of more than 3,000 folks all across the country who have a common interest in NAIC's investment methodology and who are connected through the Internet or e-mail.

More than just a fantastic source of investment ideas, the I-Club is a great networking opportunity for those wishing to compare notes about the companies they're interested in, to debate the decisions that they make when evaluating stocks, to learn, and to share learning.

A lot of what you read in this book has come from the I-Club—from folks who have learned about this investment approach on their own—or has been published there first in answer to questions that arise from people just like you.

Active I-Club participants include people such as Nancy Isaacs, an NAIC volunteer from New Jersey, who has taught more people than many a professor through her Socratic approach to learning—asking questions and demanding satisfactory answers until she is satisfied that she understands the topic completely.

It costs nothing to sign up and participate in the I-Club. Many people are simply *lurkers*, not writing a thing, just soaking up the information that's available there.

Don't overlook this resource! You can join simply by going to NAIC's Website, (*www.better-investing.org*). Unless the site has been radically changed, you will be able to just click on "I-Club List," which you'll find under "Community" on the left side of the screen.

I would be remiss if I didn't also mention NAIC's CompuServe Forum (*community.compuserve/naic*), which runs a close and closing second to the I-Club. Similar in content, but with a slightly different ambience, the forum is also a free area.

The Complete Roster of Quality Companies

This is a remarkable monthly subscription service (*www.iclub.com/isupport/roster.asp*) that my former company introduced and our successor, ICLUBcentral Inc., now provides. Where many lists will screen a database of active companies and filter out just those companies that meet a list of established criteria for the historical data, the Complete Roster of Quality Companies actually performs the analysis you will learn about in the next couple of chapters, removes irrelevant historical data, discards those companies that don't meet the quality requirements, and provides a quality rating for each surviving company on a scale from one to 10.

You can be certain that the companies appearing on this list will produce the quality results discussed in Chapters 7 through 9. You will have only to confirm the quality based on the most recent data and evaluate whether the stock is selling at a reasonable price or not, based on the things you will learn in Chapter 10. And you can do so quickly using the software that's now available.

About Tips

Most tips, regardless of their source, fall in the category of either inside information or new product potential.

If someone offers you inside information, ask yourself, "If that information is so new, exciting, and secret, how did the person who told me about it come to know about it?" (If your stockbroker offers the tip, rest assured the market has already discounted the stock.) In the case of new product information—"ABC Company is about to introduce a revolutionary new widget"—you have to ask yourself, "What percentage of current revenue can such a new product generate if that product or service is successful?" Usually the answer will be that sales of the new product will add only a tiny fraction to the current sales figures. If the company is so small that the new product would have a large impact on the company's bottom line, then the company is probably still too small or new to bother with, or the introduction of the new product is too risky to gamble on.

You can get a good idea from almost anywhere. There are as many suggestions out there as there are companies, and one might be just as good as another.

As long as you clearly understand that you should *never, never, never* buy a stock on a tip without doing your homework, you can welcome any and all tips.

Electronic Screening

There's one other means of prospecting that should be mentioned here, and that is electronic screening using a personal computer. Screening is a method of filtering a large number of companies for only those meeting the criteria that you select. You can screen on a variety of different values: sales or earnings growth rates, PE multiples, company sizes, and so on. The list of criteria varies depending upon where you go to do your screening.

The cost ranges from zero for screening on the Internet to about $250 a year for subscribing to and maintaining a database on your own computer. (Some professional screening products, with their accompanying databases, cost upward of $20,000 a year.)

Internet sources. You'll find a number of Internet sites that offer screening opportunities usually free of charge. Doug Gerlach, author of *Investor's Web Guide* and *The Complete Idiot's Guide to Online Investing*, is arguably one of today's most knowledgeable authorities on what is available on the World Wide Web for investors. He suggests the following sites as the best available today, which I offer with his comments:

> Reuters Investor Power Screener (*www.investor.reuters.com/nscreen/builder.asp*). Free membership; login required; can save your criteria for future use; criteria are customizable; can export results to Excel.

> Yahoo! Finance (*screenerfinance.yahoo.com/newscreener.html*). Java version offers 150 criteria; basic version uses HTML and fewer criteria.

> Morningstar (*screen.morningstar.com/StockSelector.html*). Premium version (for online subscribers) offers more features; free basic version is simple to use and allows screening on Morningstar Stock Grades.

> MSN Money (*moneycentral.msn.com/investor/finder/customstocks.asp*). Deluxe screener (uses ActiveX controls in Internet Explorer only) allows you to save searches and export results to Excel; combines technical and fundamental criteria.

> BusinessWeek (*prosearch.businessweek.com/businessweek/general_free_search.html*). Quick mode offers fast access to a few fundamental criteria; advanced mode delves deeper and includes momentum-based factors; allows "fuzzy" searches on values (that is, "high as possible" or "low as possible").

Screening databases and software. There are a number of desktop screening programs available as well. These provide data on a regular, subscription basis and give you the tools to filter that data for just what you want.

The most impressive of these products, in my opinion, is Stock Investor PRO (*www.aaii.com/simember/si.shtml*), made available by the American Association of Individual Investors (AAII), another nonprofit organization whose mission, as is NAIC's, is to educate individual investors and enhance their ability to make sound investment decisions on their own. Whereas Internet sites that permit screening generally have only a few key criteria on which you may screen, Stock Investor PRO offers as many as 1,500 predetermined variables, plus the ability to create your own.

Another product that has come into its own and matured since this book was first published is ICLUBcentral's *NAIC Stock Prospector*. Designed specifically around NAIC criteria, this program requires the use of NAIC's Online Premium Service (OPS) data, which is available at little or no cost to NAIC members, and permits screening not only on the desired criteria but on rankings for those criteria within industries. At a price of only $99 for NAIC members, this product is an inexpensive and effective approach to screening for good quality stocks.

Let's Take Stock of   What to Look for and Where to Find It

You Don't Want

▶ Companies that are too small or young.

▶ Companies that are too big or old.

▶ Companies that aren't "in business" yet (that is, companies that are earning no money).

▶ Companies that are in businesses you don't understand—or care to understand.

You Do Want

> ➤ Companies whose sales are growing year to year, consistent with company size, and at a rate that can produce satisfactory earnings growth.

> ➤ Companies whose earnings are growing year to year at a rate that will allow them to double every five years.

You can find information about good candidates almost anywhere, from the newspaper to your hair stylist. Your library and the Internet are two very fruitful places to find both good candidates and the data you will need for your studies.

Just don't buy anything on a tip! Consider no investment until you have studied the company using the methods that you will learn in detail in the next several chapters.

Chapter 7

Evaluating Company Quality

T
o buy a good stock, you only need to know if the company is a
good-quality company and if the price you have to pay for its
stock is reasonable. *If you can tell the difference between a straight
and a crooked line and whether it slopes up or down, you can tell nearly
everything you need to know about a company's quality.* It's really that simple!

A good-quality company is one whose growth, upon which you rely to
increase the value of your investment, is strong and stable, and one in
which management's *efficiency* will enable it to continue that satisfactory
growth. Both of these elements can be represented by lines on charts
whose technamental interpretation requires no more than the simple skills
I cite in the first paragraph. In this chapter and the next, you'll learn how
to quickly evaluate the strength and stability of a company's growth. In
Chapter 9, you'll learn to evaluate management's ability to sustain it.

The Charts

Technamental analysis uses two kinds of charts to evaluate growth and
efficiency. The first is a growth chart that is known technically as a semilog chart. This is what you'll use to analyze the quality of sales and earnings growth. The other is a simple linear chart you can use to look at
management's efficiency.

You can generate these charts painlessly on a computer using either electronic or printed data, or you can plot the charts by hand. If you have a computer, the disk accompanying this book will create them for you, as will any of the software reviewed in Appendix B.

The illustrations in this book were created quite easily using either the computer program, *Take $tock*, available from ICLUBcentral Inc, using NAIC's Online Premium Service data (provided by S&P Compustat), or using Microsoft's Excel spreadsheet program.

If you're not a computer user, you can still do what's required using either the Technamental Stock Study Worksheet or using NAIC's Stock Selection Guide, available from NAIC, which is similar. (In the first edition of *Take Stock*, I devoted many pages to doing this work by hand. At this point, because it is both more convenient and because computers are more ubiquitous, I will not do so. However, if you are interested in the details about preparing these forms manually, using the data from the *Value Line Survey* or Standard & Poor's tear sheets, drop me a note at *etraub@financialiteracy.us* and I will tell you how to obtain a small booklet that contains the information that was in the earlier edition.)

Whether you are a computer user or not, it's still a good idea to obtain a business calculator. You can get one at your local discount office supply store for around $25. One of the most popular is Texas Instruments' BA-35. You need one that has four keys: "PV" (present value), "FV" (future value), "i%" (percent), and "N" (number of periods). It will also have a key that calculates the result. It will be labeled "CPT" or something similar. These keys are used to solve problems involving the time value of money. To solve for any of the four values, you simply enter the other three and press the "CPT" key to compute the fourth. With such a calculator, you can quickly determine compounded growth rates and rates of return and do all of the other calculations required for your technamental analysis. Where such calculations are necessary, I'll indicate which keys to use.

Charting Growth

Chapter 5 was devoted to learning about the nature of growth, where it comes from, and how companies from Lucy's Lemonade Stand to General Electric generate growth in sales and earnings. That discussion gave you insight into the character and quality of growth.

You learned in Chapter 6 how to find a good candidate for consideration. And now you're ready to scrutinize that candidate's growth more closely to see if it has the character—the stability and strength—to be a good enough company to invest in.

You're interested in *compounded* growth as opposed to simple, linear growth. When the growth is compounded, you start with $1.00 and it grows 15 percent during the first year. You then have $1.15 at the end of the year. The following year $1.15, not the original $1.00, grows 15 percent. See Figure 7.1 to understand the effect. As you can see, compounded growth at a little less than 15 percent will double your money in five years.

$1 growing at 15%	Linear	Compounded
Starting amount	$1.00	$1.00
End of year 1	1.15	1.15
End of year 2	1.30	1.32
End of year 3	1.45	1.52
End of year 4	1.60	1.75
End of year 5	1.75	2.01

Figure 7.1. Difference Between Linear (Simple) Growth and Compounded Growth

You can see from this chart just why it doesn't pay to pull money out of your account if you don't have to. The "Linear" column shows what will happen if you withdraw your gain each year. Leaving your earnings there will allow compounding to work its magic, doubling your money in five years.

Technamental analysis of sales and earnings growth means that you plot and literally look at that growth to appraise it, so you should know what a growth chart is and how you'll use it.

Some people have a knack for looking at a row or column of numbers, interpreting the numbers, and drawing conclusions from them.

However, if you're like most people, when you look at a relationship between one set of numbers and another, it hardly sticks out as the proverbial damaged digit. So it doesn't do a whole lot of good to deal just with the raw numbers. You need a better way to visualize the numbers' significance. This is where a chart or graph is invaluable.

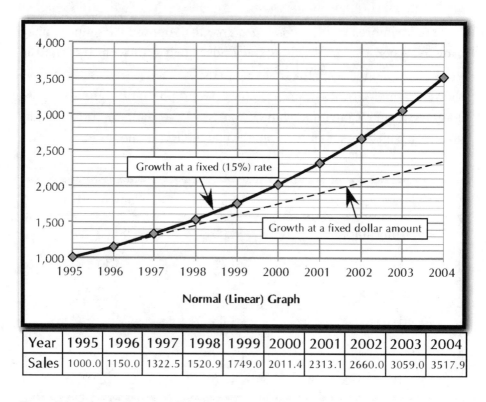

Year	1995	1996	1997	1998	1999	2000	2001	2002	2003	2004
Sales	1000.0	1150.0	1322.5	1520.9	1749.0	2011.4	2313.1	2660.0	3059.0	3517.9

Figure 7.2. Sales Growing at 15%, Plotted on a Linear Chart

At the bottom of Figure 7.2 there is a table with sales figures for 10 years.

Above the table the data are plotted on a regular (linear) graph. The sales figures (in millions of dollars) are listed along the left side (on the *Y*, or vertical, axis), and the years are shown along the bottom (on the *X*, or horizontal, axis).

This is one picture that's worth a thousand words. It should be obvious that you can best analyze growth when you can actually see it. But the chart tells you little about the rate of growth. Because the bold line curves higher each year, you might think the rate of growth is increasing, but, in fact, it's not. The rate of growth is the same each year.

If sales had increased at the same *dollar amount* (in this case, $150 million) each year rather than growing at the same rate, the line that depicts sales growth would be straight, as the dotted line is in the illustration. Although the dollar-amount line slopes up, the *rate* of growth is actually declining.

In the case of a linear chart such as the one in Figure 7.2, it's easy to read the sales values because they are evenly spaced along the left side. But it's not easy to interpret the rate of growth except to say that the line climbs as it goes from left to right, indicating an increase—some growth.

You're interested in seeing how a company's growth *rate* fares. You're looking for a business that maintains a fairly consistent record of growth; it must increase its *increase* each year. This is the *compounded* growth I spoke of previously.

It's difficult for a company to maintain a steady growth rate forever. According to the *law of large numbers*, the bigger the company gets—that is, the bigger the revenues become—the greater the revenues required to sustain that growth rate. (But then you only ask the company to sustain its rate for the duration of your lifetime.) Look at the same data plotted on a semilog, or growth, chart in Figure 7.3.

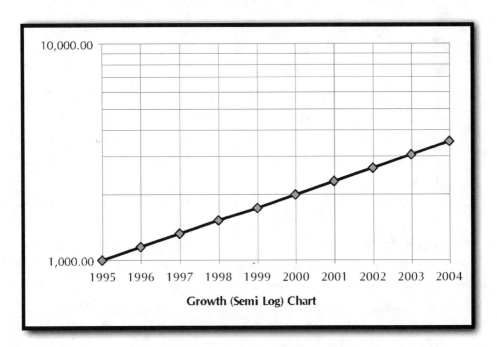

Figure 7.3. The Same Data, Shown on a Growth (Semilog) Chart

Again, sales in the example have grown steadily at 15 percent. The plotted data now show up as a straight line. The obvious advantages of using a growth chart are that a constant growth rate is easy to see and that changes in that rate can be spotted at a glance.

Any increase in the rate of growth will appear clearly as an increase in the slope of the line, and any decrease will reduce the line's slope. When you use a growth chart, the actual dollar amounts might be more difficult to determine but, because you're interested only in analyzing the rate of growth, this display is much more meaningful to you.

An additional advantage of using a growth chart is that sales figures in the billions of dollars can be plotted on the same chart as earnings figures in dollars and cents, so rates of growth can easily be compared. It makes little difference whether the number is 1 cent or $1 billion; it can be plotted on the same line on the same chart.

In summary, we use a semilog, or growth, chart to analyze growth because:

➤ A straight line depicts compounded growth at a consistent rate.

➤ A change in the rate of growth is easily recognized.

➤ A growth chart is useful for comparing growth rates, even the growth rate of sales revenue in the billions with that of earnings per share in dollars and cents.

➤ You can fit more data on a smaller chart. Within three logarithmic scales or decades, for example, you can plot from $1 million to $1 billion, or from 10 cents to $10. Not too many companies are capable of growing more than that in 10 or 15 years.

Analyzing Growth

When analyzing the trends in sales and earnings, look first at the general trend. Does the line slope upward? Look to see how steep or flat the sales and earnings lines are—the steeper the lines are, the stronger the growth. Of course, you can't tell the precise rate of growth just by looking. But you can get a general impression of a company's history of solid growth and its potential to continue being a strong-growth company.

Jim Jubak, now senior markets editor for Microsoft Network's Money Central and then the senior financial editor of *Worth* magazine, referred to the growth chart in his book *The Worth Guide to Electronic Investing* (Harper Collins, 1996) as "perhaps the best single fundamental tool now available for grouping the character of a growth stock." Probably the most important benefit that you can glean from your inspection of the growth chart of a company is that you will get a feel for the predictability of its growth.

The first key to successful investing, and the easiest task in your technamental analysis, is to recognize predictable growth. The only skill you require for this purpose is being able to tell a straight line from a crooked one.

The sun comes up each morning. That's certainly predictable. Your coworker brings a peanut butter sandwich to work today just as he has every day for the past year. Odds are that he'll bring one in tomorrow, too. The more regular the behavior, the more predictable it is. And so it is with a company's growth. If your candidate's sales have been growing at a steady 15 percent every year for the past 10 years as in Figure 7.3, you can be reasonably confident that it will do pretty much the same for at least the next year or two.

You can usually tell enough just by looking at a growth chart of a company's sales and earnings history to know whether it's going to be worth the trouble to continue studying that company. Because constant growth rates are shown as straight lines, you can tell at a glance whether growth is steady and positive.

Of course, you will rarely find growth to be perfectly steady. Rates vary from year to year, and in some cases the lines are punctuated by severe peaks or valleys.

(Growth from a zero or negative beginning value is mathematically meaningless, so a growth chart cannot display a zero or negative value.) When a company has had a really bad year, producing no earnings or experiencing a loss, that data will disappear off the bottom of the chart because there's no place to plot it. The dip will show as a break in the lines that connect the points on the chart. And that's okay because we're not interested so much in *how much* a company lost in a given year as we are in the simple fact that it *did* lose money.

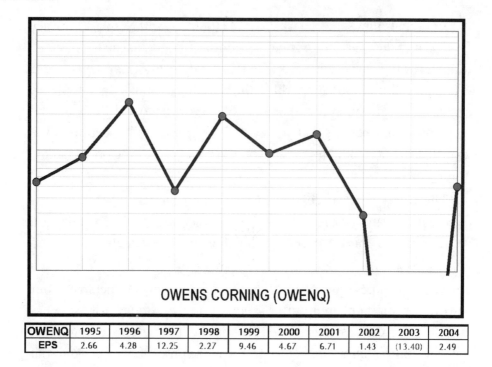

OWENS CORNING (OWENQ)

OWENQ	1995	1996	1997	1998	1999	2000	2001	2002	2003	2004
EPS	2.66	4.28	12.25	2.27	9.46	4.67	6.71	1.43	(13.40)	2.49

Figure 7.4. Owens Corning (OWENQ) Earnings Growth]

Figure 7.4 shows the earnings of Owens Corning (OWENQ) during the period from 1995 through 2004. This company's growth is obviously inadequate and unpredictable.

You can easily see that Owens Corning made good money in 1995. Its earnings grew at a good rate in 1996 and even more rapidly in 1997. However, it slipped in 1998, bounced back some in 1999 but declined more than 50 percent in 2000, came back some in 2001, then took a tumble in 2002, lost money in 2003, and finally became profitable again in 2004, though barely exceeding 1998's earnings.

It's obvious that Owens Corning's earnings have declined over the 10 years displayed. In view of what you already know about you're looking for, it's a no-brainer to decide with only a glance that you're not interested, isn't it?

I suppose it could be said that the longer it takes to describe what you see on the chart, the less desirable the company is. For instance, compare the paragraph before the last with a description of the chart for Bed Bath and Beyond (BBBY) in Figure 7.5: "Earnings have grown at about 30 percent for the past 10 years." Here is your first glance at "monotonous excellence."

The more erratic the growth (that is, the more crooked the line representing that growth), the less confidence you will have in predicting whether growth will continue and at what rate, especially if in some years the company didn't grow at all.

Sales growth should be the most predictable of the statistics you analyze because very few short-term factors impact it—especially for a company that has annual sales of more than $100 million.

The sudden onslaught of unexpected competition, a serious product failure, a major disaster, or a successful class-action lawsuit against a company are among the factors that can make a noticeable difference in sales growth. Aside from such major events, however, changes in the growth rate of sales are subtle and take place over a long period of time. They are brought about by less-obvious factors such as a less-than-successful marketing campaign for a single product, a decrease in standards or morale in the sales force, or long-term changes in management.

Earnings growth is apt to be a lot less predictable than sales growth, because it's affected not only by all of the factors that influence sales growth but also by all of the additional things that chop away at the profit before it reaches the bottom line. Major changes in the cost of producing the product or service can take place from year to year, even from quarter to quarter, as can changes to the company's fixed costs, taxes, or the number of shares among which the profits are divided. All of these items impact earnings per share.

If you can see steady growth in earnings as well as sales, then you can be confident about predicting a company's future growth, but if the graph of year-to-year earnings looks to be a roller coaster, you won't be able to muster up that degree of confidence. Management that's not capable of keeping expenses from fluctuating widely from period to period likely lacks the skill for which you're looking.

The *company's* success is based upon its ability to make earnings grow. *Your* success will be based upon how well you're able to forecast that growth. So you're interested in companies with steady, predictable growth.

And you need only recognize whether the growth is stable enough for you to be comfortable—whether the line is crooked or relatively straight.

The bottom line? Looking at companies with patterns that swing wildly from high growth to none, it's easy to see that they just don't have it together, no matter what promises management may make in its annual report. Saw teeth in the growth chart are a raucous Klaxon that warn you to stay away! You're looking for companies with charts that come closer to monotonous excellence than the others you can find.

What if the company is growing somewhat erratically but exceptionally fast? In most cases, the fastest growers do not have enough experience to stabilize or produce a track record you can rely on. You might highlight a company that bears watching for the future, but rapid growth, if erratic, is not necessarily the sign of a good prospect—at least for the moment. On the other hand, you won't turn your nose up at a company whose growth is both rapid and stable.

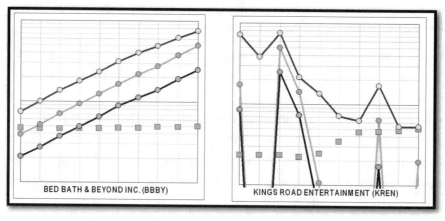

Figure 7.5. Bed Bath and Beyond (BBBY) and Kings Road Entertainment (KREN)

In Figure 7.5 are a couple of charts from real companies illustrating the extremes of what we're talking about. Which company would you want to buy? Of course, the companies you look at will fall somewhere between the two extremes, but wouldn't it be nice if all of the companies you came across had growth charts resembling that of Bed Bath and Beyond? One way to make that happen is to use a screening program to filter out those that don't. You might also want to take a look at the Complete Roster of Quality Companies that ICLUBcentral offers on its

Website (*www.iclub.com*). The charts of all of the companies displayed there should be "suitable for framing" as far as the quality issues are concerned. (See Figure 9.4 at the end of Chapter 9 for a partial gallery of companies that the Complete Roster of Quality Companies identified as being good candidates.)

Deciding how straight the lines must be is a matter of developing your personal comfort zone. The best way to judge the degree of crookedness of a line is to visualize a straight line representing the general trend of the growth (see Figure 7.6). Unless you can draw a line with a ruler that touches or comes fairly close to most of the points—at least for the most recent five years—you should probably find another company to study.

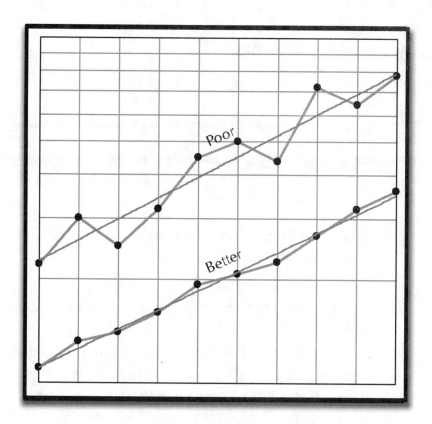

Figure 7.6. Using a Straight Line to Assess Degree of Crookedness

Until you gain experience and get a better feel for analyzing growth, you should stick with the admonition "if in doubt, throw it out." You may miss some good buys, but you won't be tempted to purchase stocks you shouldn't.

Applying What You've Learned

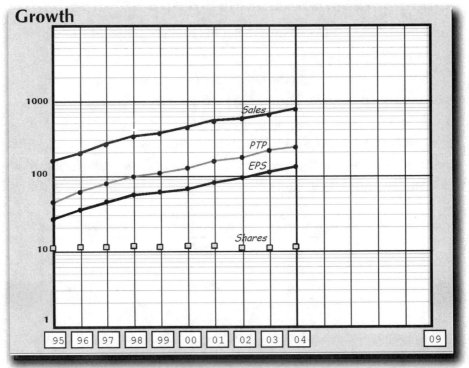

Figure 7.7. Growth Chart for ABC Company

Let's assess ABC Company's growth. Looking at the chart in Figure 7.7, what's your first impression?

1. Are the lines representing sales and earnings relatively straight, especially for the most recent five years, or do they zigzag from year to year?

    Although there is a slight droop, there are no erratic swings from strong growth to flat growth and back. So you would have to say that ABC Company's growth is stable. (Compare this chart with the Owings Corning chart in Figure 7.4.)

2. Is the slope from left to right positive or negative, strong or slight?

    It's easy to see that the line slopes upward. As to how strongly it slopes, it would be difficult to tell the difference between 13-percent and 17-percent growth. You can get a feel for how strong the growth rate is by comparing the most recent year's approximate value with that of five years before. If value has doubled in the last five years, growth is at least 15 percent. In Figure 7.9 the most recent earnings figure is about 130, and the figure for five years ago is about 60, so ABC Company is experiencing a growth rate of at least 15 percent.

3. Do the sales and earnings lines climb steadily as they go from left to right?

    Well, they did sag a little for a while. But then they settled into a comfortably stable straight upslope, which they have sustained for the last five years or more. So although growth slowed initially, it's been pretty steady for a significant period.

    You could feel comfortable forecasting that ABC Company will grow at or close to its recent rate. This business warrants further study.

Now that wasn't so hard, was it? This information is valuable and has already made a substantial contribution to your assessment of quality.

Not all companies have the same fine characteristics as this one, of course. The good news is that most of those you should reject will scream caution to you from their growth charts.

Evaluating Strength of Growth

Presumably, when you first considered a company as a candidate, it met your requirements for sales and earnings growth—at least so far as a perfunctory look at the company's chart could peg it. You've confirmed this qualitatively because the line on the growth chart does slope up at an apparently good rate.

Now you need to know if the company has been growing fast enough. In the past, has it met your requirement to double your money every five years? If so, then it might be able to do so in the future.

To measure the strength of growth, you will need a line that sums up the trend of growth over the period for which you have data. The computer can do this for you using what is known in statistics as the *least squares* formula to accurately calculate the position of a *trend line* that lies as close as possible to all of the points it's intended to describe. You can approximate the same thing visually with a ruler. This line will not only measure the relevant historical growth rate to determine if it is sufficient, but it will provide you with a starting point from which to construct a reasonable forecast of future growth. This, in the final analysis, is the reason for studying history.

Eliminating Irrelevant History

Before a trend line can be useful to you, however, you will want to eliminate any outliers, irrelevant historical data reflecting events or conditions that have occurred in the past and are unlikely to occur again and that make no contribution toward your forecast of the future.

Including extraneous data in your measurements and calculations can easily skew the results enough to give you a false picture—most likely and most damaging, an excessively optimistic one. You should focus only on relevant history because you want to increase your odds of being right. If you take pains to be conservative, erring on the cautious side, you're far less likely to be disappointed. After all, isn't successful investing a matter of keeping disappointment to a manageable minimum?

Briefly, outliers—irrelevant data—consist of two types:

1. *Spikes*. One-time events, usually bad, that show up as a significant deviation from the rest of the data.

2. *Early rapid growth*. Unsustainable growth that occurred in the past and is no longer likely to continue.

By avoiding companies whose growth is erratic and selecting only those whose lines have no major peaks and valleys, you will have disposed of businesses with spikes in their history. However, you'll want to be aware of the latter type of outlier because, even though early rapid growth doesn't necessarily disqualify a company from your consideration, it can definitely throw off your forecasts (see Figure 7.8 on page 119).

Getting rid of outliers is simple enough. If you're using a computer, your program will allow you to eliminate the earlier data from the calculation of the trend with a few clicks of the mouse.

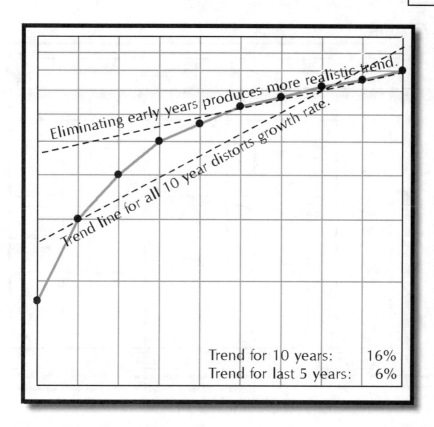

Figure 7.8. Eliminating Early Rapid Growth

Once you've eliminated early years and you're satisfied with the remaining data, you can read the growth rate for the remaining data displayed on the computer screen.

I would encourage you to make use of the CD at the back of the book from this point on.

Let's use ABC Company as an example again. In Figure 7.9 on page 120 the trend line eliminates the first four years as outliers and fits nicely along the most recent six years.

The 1999 earnings were 1.32. In 1994, five years earlier, they were 0.61. If you plug those numbers into your trusty calculator (FV = 1.32; PV = .61; N = 5), you'll arrive at a growth rate of 16.7 percent, more than enough to have doubled your money over that period. (The computer measures the precise slope of the line and comes up with 16.8. Close enough!)

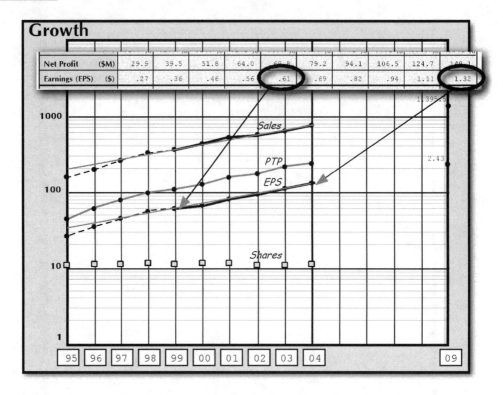

Net Profit ($M)	29.9	39.5	51.8	64.0	69.8	79.2	94.1	106.5	124.7	148
Earnings (EPS) ($)	.27	.36	.46	.56	.61	.69	.82	.94	1.11	1.32

Figure 7.9. Measuring Growth for ABC Company

Requirements for Growth

Let's take a look now at just how strong a company needs to grow its sales and earnings to qualify as a potential investment.

Sales Growth

Because your goal is to double your investment's value every five years, it would seem reasonable that you should discard any company that isn't capable of generating sales growth at a minimum of 15 percent every year.

However, that isn't necessarily realistic; nor is it really necessary. Revenue growth can vary with the size of a company. The bigger the company, the smaller the growth rate you should require. Your goal is to have a *portfolio* whose average return is 15 percent or better. This doesn't require that all of the companies in it do that well.

120

Growth is bound to slow down as a good company grows larger. Small companies early in their life cycles grow at a very rapid clip because it's relatively easy to add new customers, find new markets, and grow sales from a small base. It's simple math.

In the interest of diversification, you're going to put some of your investment into larger companies to provide stability and strength when times are tough.

And you're going to be willing to sacrifice a little return on your investment to buy that security.

Most mature companies, after reaching the point where they can no longer make as much money as they once could by reinvesting in their own growth, will begin to reward their stockholders with dividends, which make a contribution toward the total return. A 10-percent growth in earnings combined with a 3-percent dividend, for example, would produce a 13-percent total return, which is better than the S&P 500 has produced on average since its inception. And more and more large companies are capable of doing better than that. You may not double your money every five years through growth in the price of the stock, but you might make up some of the difference in dividend income. The stability and security of having an established business to serve as a sea anchor in stormy times could well be worth some sacrifice in the return on your investment.

Depending upon the size of the company, therefore, you should expect annual sales growth rates that vary from a low of about 7 percent to a high of about 20 percent. For a large, well-established company that has sales well in excess of the $4 billion mark, a growth rate of as little as 7 percent might be perfectly acceptable. At the other end of the spectrum, a newer company well into its explosive growth period should show double-digit growth. Although growth rates above 20 percent can't go on forever, you'll want to look for high growth rates as compensation for the increased risk. The more risky, fast-growing companies are needed to balance the slower-growing large companies in your portfolio and contribute to an average growth of your investments of around 15 percent or better.

Some of the faster-growing companies will fall by the wayside, to be sure, but the successful smaller companies will eventually grow to become big ones. And you're going along for that long-term ride!

Figure 7.10 provides a rough guideline for the kinds of sales growth rates for which I suggest you look. A growth rate in the light area of the chart is acceptable. For example, if a company's sales for the current year are in the neighborhood of $300 million, you would look for a growth rate of better than 12 percent. For a company with $1 billion in sales, you would want at least 10 percent.

Our guidelines tell us to look for a minimum of 7-percent growth in sales for a large company and at least 12-percent growth for a small company. Preferably a small company will have growth of 15 percent or more if we are to double our money every five years.

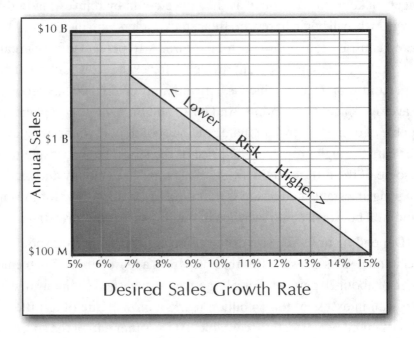

Figure 7.10. Trading Risk for Reward

Earnings Growth

Because you depend upon earnings growth to double your investment every five years, as a rule you'd like to see 15 percent. There are several rationales for accepting something less, however. First of all, as I said previously, it's not reasonable to expect every stock in your portfolio to produce returns at that rate. Your goal is for your portfolio, as a whole, to produce 15 percent. So, again, if you're looking at a larger company, you can settle for a lower rate as long as you keep the average high.

If sales growth is adequate and your first impression of this company is favorable, but earnings growth is just a bit short, continue your study. Your underlying interest is in the total return that the company can generate. It might just be that the current price of the stock is far enough below the fair price that you can realize a price appreciation of 15 percent or greater even with a smaller growth in earnings.

The current price (and therefore the PE) might offer some room for *PE expansion*: If you buy a stock at a price below its fair price, you can expect that the multiple of earnings will grow somewhat as the earnings grow. Of course, this is what the traders and short-term speculators all rely on, all the time. I'm just suggesting that, if a company's earnings growth is a little short of your normal mark, a small component of PE expansion might make it possible to acquire a bargain.

Checking Quarterly Sales Growth

You're now at the point in your consideration of ABC Company where you can again exercise your prerogative to go on or to abandon the study. Your computer or calculator has told you that after you eliminate the data for the first four years, relevant sales growth for ABC Company is about 15 percent and earnings have stabilized at about 16.7 percent. So you're satisfied that both sales and earnings display satisfactory growth. At $757 million dollars, ABC Company's sales put the company in the lower part of the midsize companies. Twelve percent is the lower sales-growth limit for that category, so sales growth is just fine, and earnings growth is nicely above the desired 15 percent.

There's one more thing you might want to do before you go on to look at management's ability to sustain this desirable record. You might want to see if anything has happened recently to alter your opinion about the company's growth.

To do this, compare the sales figures for the sum of the most recent four quarters with the sales figures for the sum of the four quarters prior to that. Do the same for earnings. The percentage increases for both sales and earnings should be close to the growth at which you arrived with your annual data.

The computer will do this nicely for you, but some computer programs don't display the entire four quarters. You may have to settle for just a comparison between the most recent quarter and the same quarter in the previous year. The advantage of using the entire trailing four quarters is that it will reduce the effect of a single hiccup and smooth out the numbers.

If you're a new investor, negative figures here, or figures that are significantly lower than annual growth rates, should tell you "no." Period.

If you're an experienced investor and have been doing technamental analysis for a while, you may decide to do some research, exploring the Internet, perhaps, to find out why the poor performance occurred and to assess whether the reasons are long term or short term in nature. If the problem is long term, you should not invest. If the problem's only a hiccup, you may decide to give management another quarter or two to correct it.

Remember that there are more candidates out there, so you shouldn't get hung up on any one stock just because you happen to like its story.

Let's look at the quarterly performance for ABC Company in Figure 7.11.

	Quarterly Sales					Quarterly Earnings (EPS)				
	Qtr 2	Qtr 3	Qtr 4	Qtr 1	TTM	Qtr 2	Qtr 3	Qtr 4	Qtr 1	TTM
Last year	156.6	161.0	184.3	176.7	678.6	.27	.28	.30	.30	1.15
This year	183.3	192.3	205.1	192.2	772.9	.32	.33	.37	.35	1.37
% Change	17.0%	19.4%	11.3 %	8.8%	13.9%	18.5%	17.9%	23.3%	16.7%	19.1%

Figure 7.11. Quarterly Performance

(Note that the most recent reported quarter is the first quarter of the year 2005. Quarters are listed chronologically beginning with the second quarter of 2003.) Here you can see that sales growth, quarter to quarter, has been declining somewhat over the past few quarters.

Some companies are very much impacted by seasonal change, retailers especially because of the holiday activity. Although that seasonal effect is easy to see from quarter to quarter in the actual sales figures, it does not affect year-to-year growth, the percent change from the previous year's quarter that you're analyzing. So a decline in sales over the course of the year may not be meaningful, but a decline in growth from year to year could be.

Quarterly performance doesn't carry quite the weight that annual (or trailing four-quarter) data do because anything can happen in a single quarter and never recur. However, it can be a good warning bell for you. You might find it prudent to give the company one more quarter to see if it can reverse the trend. However, I don't believe that these figures have declined enough to be alarming, and growth for the trailing four quarters is still well above our benchmark.

Not Minutes, Moments!

It's taken a long time to read about analyzing growth, but what you've read about will take only moments to apply. Once your data is entered into your computer, you can see the quality of growth at a glance, eliminate the required outliers with a mouse click or two, and read the growth rates right off the screen.

Let's Take Stock of **What You Know About Evaluating Company Quality**

> ➤ To be suitable as an investment, a company must be of good quality and have a reasonable stock price.

> ➤ The first technamental assessment of a company's quality is the analysis of its sales and earnings growth.

> ➤ Growth is best viewed using a growth (semi log) chart, which depicts a consistent rate of growth as a straight line and permits you to see at a glance whether growth is positive and predictable.

> ➤ The straighter the line showing growth, the more predictable it is, and the better the candidate.

> ➤ The steeper the slope, the stronger growth is, and the better the candidate.

➤ It's important to eliminate irrelevant data in order to properly measure historical growth and to provide a reasonable starting point for estimating future growth.

➤ Stronger growth is required of smaller companies than of larger ones to make up for the difference in stability and risk.

➤ You should check recently reported data to ensure that nothing has happened to undermine an otherwise good track record.

➤ Once you've become accustomed to the process, it should take less than a minute to analyze growth.

In the next chapter I'll take you on a tour of some of the more common growth scenarios you're likely to come across.

CHAPTER 8

Variations on the Growth Theme

The charts in this chapter illustrate some typical patterns of growth, both good and bad, that you'll come across in your studies. The purpose is for you to see the reasons why each pattern is good or bad so that, when you encounter similar situations in your own research, you'll find them familiar and will know what they mean. Don't try to memorize anything. Instead, try to understand how the pictures translate into numbers and vice versa—what these patterns of growth mean and why they're acceptable or not. Bear in mind that these charts are caricatures—exaggerations of what you will typically find—to make the conditions a bit more identifiable. We'll look at each pattern and discuss its significance. After that I'll offer a few examples of actual companies so you can see how the patterns look in real life.

Note that I have drawn the trend lines in gray on each chart. This should help you to view the relevant historical growth realistically.

As I was writing this book, it was when I reached this point in the text that I dreamed up the term *technamental*. I looked at what I was doing and realized that I was charting, the favorite pastime of technical analysts, and even calling different types of patterns by different names just as they do.

But this process differs from technical analysis in a very noteworthy way. We are looking at what the company's *operations* did, not what the price of the stock and volume of shares traded did. Patterns of growth are significant because they can be used to predict what's coming, whereas stock price movement can't. These examples are intended to help you understand what actually happens in the life of a company, not the meaningless meanderings of the company's stock price in the short-term market. This is a crucial distinction, and it's the reason that I have chosen the term *technamental* to describe this approach. What we will be doing amounts to a technical analysis of the fundamentals.

The Charts

Each chart displays, from top to bottom, sales, pretax profit, and earnings, respectively. If you do your charting manually, you may later find it interesting to plot some other data—shares outstanding, for example. But for now this is all you need.

Keep in mind that *sales growth drives pretax profit growth*, and pretax profit is a function of the expenses paid to produce the products or services and generate those sales.

Pretax profit growth, in turn, *drives net profit growth* (which is not displayed), and net profit is what remains after taxes are paid.

Finally, earnings per share results from dividing the net profit by the number of shares outstanding. Therefore, *the number of shares can have a significant effect on earnings*. A reduction in shares will increase earnings per share, and an increase in shares will reduce EPS.

You can distinguish trends in the profit margin by viewing changes in the space between the pretax profit and sales lines. An increase in the size of that space indicates an increase in the portion of sales that goes to expenses—hence a decrease in the profit margin. The narrower the space becomes, the smaller the percentage going to expenses and the greater the profit margin. Thus, you can tell by looking at the lines on the chart whether a change in earnings growth is caused by changes in the profit margin or by increases or decreases in the number of shares outstanding.

Although you only need to go as far as I suggested in Chapter 7, rejecting all companies that don't exhibit strong, reasonably straight up-slopes, you may find it fun and interesting to interpret the dynamics between the lines. (You'll find a more detailed discussion of these variations in Chapter 13.) As you study these charts, you should begin to see and understand the relationship between the sales, pretax profit, and earnings lines—and between these and the squares representing the outstanding shares.

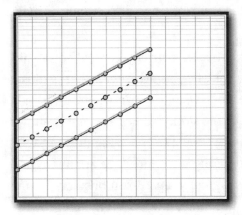
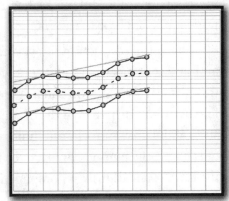

Figure 8.1. Monotonous Excellence   *Figure 8.2. The Motorcycle*

Monotonous Excellence (Figure 8 .1)

All of your companies should look as the *Monotonous Excellence* chart does! Companies whose management can maintain "railroad tracks"—straight, parallel lines—are highly desirable. This is the kind of pattern you will look for in all of your holdings.

Obviously, perfection is hard to find. So, your investment experience will likely include small compromises. The steeper the slope, the more forgiving you might be about stability—you'll swap a little zigzag in the line for faster growth.

The smaller the company, the faster the growth and the less predictable the fundamentals might be. Of course, the larger and slower-growing the company, the more demanding you'll be in terms of predictability. But don't stray too far from the Monotonous Excellence model, especially when you first start out.

The Motorcycle (Figure 8.2)

The *Motorcycle* pattern is not strictly cyclical, as its name seems to imply. I named it because the prime examples of cyclical companies are the motor makers—the automobile manufacturers. Strictly cyclical companies are those whose lines look like a roller coaster and whose high and low points seem always to be about the same. They usually depend upon a surge in economic good times to overcome the misery of the bad times. Stay away from strictly cyclical companies, because you aren't interested in timing your investments by keeping track of when a cycle may or may not be at its high or low point.

There is a distinction, however, between a strictly cyclical company and one that has the kind of cyclical or undulating growth that is illustrated in Figure 8.2. You can test the slope visually by drawing your trend line between the peaks of the cycles. If the slope is steep enough to show substantial growth from one point in the cycle to the same point in the next cycle, the company may, over the long term, produce adequate returns. A cyclical-growth company is typically a well-run business in an industry that is affected by the rise and fall of the economy. Its growth usually ratchets up when its industry takes a beating and it is strong enough to acquire its weaker competitors' business. When the industry comes back into favor, the cyclical-growth company shoots ahead of where it was before.

As a new investor, you should treat a cyclical-growth company as any other. If the growth during the down phase becomes flat or negative as illustrated here, you should exercise caution. If, however, there is constant growth that varies in magnitude, if the cycle is predictable, and if growth doesn't fall too far below the desired growth rate in the down years, you might consider making the company a candidate.

Companies with patterns such as this are best purchased after comparing them with their peers in their industry (see Chapter 11).

The Bow and Arrow (Figure 8.3)

The "bow" part of the *Bow and Arrow* pattern is easy to see. Its path appears as a trajectory. If you were to draw a trend line that describes the growth for the entire period displayed, it would resemble the string on that bow (as illustrated by the dotted gray lines in figure 8.3). This is

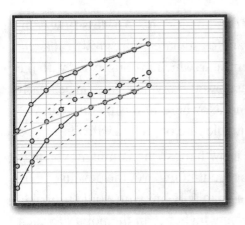

Figure 8.3. The Bow and Arrow

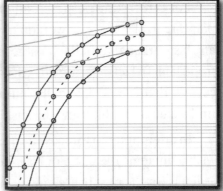

Figure 8.4. The Arrowless Bow

typical of a company that is fairly early in its life cycle and has been enjoying superior but unsustainable growth. Some companies experience extraordinary growth longer than others, and what may be sustainable in one industry may not be in another.

Bow and Arrow companies show promise, but you must be careful not to measure historical growth by the "string." This is a good example of historical irrelevance. The early growth is irrelevant when you are considering a prospective growth rate for the future. As you can see by comparing the gray trend lines in the illustration, you should disregard those early years when measuring historical growth.

But how about the "arrow"? That's what I've called the part where the growth has settled down to a sustainable rate. As you can see in Figure 8.3, the last five years' growth falls in a fairly straight line. The fact that growth has stabilized should enhance your confidence in forecasting: In the future this company should grow at a rate not too far below its growth rate for the past five years.

The Arrowless Bow (Figure 8.4)

As the name implies, the *Arrowless Bow* is a bow without an arrow. Sure enough, in this chart you can see no settling down to a straight line. As with the Bow and Arrow pattern, this is typical of a company that is early in its life cycle and continues to grow at a rapid but declining rate. But the Arrowless Bow company has not yet settled down to a rate that's sustainable.

131

For forecasting purposes, all of the data for an Arrowless Bow company are irrelevant. You wouldn't want to estimate future growth at a rate any faster than that of the most recent year, which I've suggested with the trend line. In fact, because growth has slowed every year, you can be nearly certain that the decline will continue. Nowhere in this picture can you find a clue about how low the sustainable rate of growth will be.

In attempting to forecast future growth for such a company, you may wish to imagine the curve or trajectory continuing over the next five years as it has for the past five. Drawing an imaginary line, you would probably not wish to forecast future earnings any higher than the point at which that line crosses the fifth year out. This is still speculation, however, because you have no history to indicate that this company is capable of sustaining its growth at an acceptable rate.

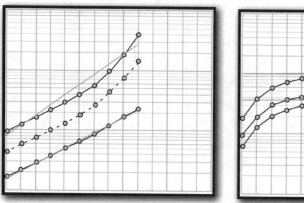

Figure 8.5. The Rocket   Figure 8.6. The Flatliner

The Rocket (Figure 8.5)

The *Rocket* is so called because it gathers momentum after liftoff. This company's growth, instead of suffering the customary decline, actually accelerates. This phenomenon is usually associated with acquisitions because it's very rare for a company of any size to introduce new products or create new markets that can generate sufficient organic growth to produce this kind of growth-rate increase. Goodness knows, it's difficult enough to perpetuate a rate, much less to increase it in the normal course of business!

When you see a Rocket pattern, you can often confirm that acquisitions are the source of growth. Look for a telltale decline in earnings growth as pretax profits are growing parallel with sales. This results from issuing shares to consummate the acquisitions, which tends to dilute and so reduce the earnings per share.

As the gray trend line implies, your assessment of historical growth should probably be based on the composite growth for the entire period. Surely the most recent growth is not sustainable for obvious reasons. It might even be more fitting to eliminate the most recent years as irrelevant and go back to the earlier years to measure what is sustainable. Be very careful that you don't overestimate future growth because of this kind of pattern. Growth from acquisitions is hardly sustainable.

The Flatliner (Figure 8.6)

The "heartbeat" of the *Flatliner* company has slowed down and stopped. This business is dead! Sales and earnings are flat and have been so for a long time. Though the Flatliner company is not losing money, it shows no potential for growth and should be avoided. The pattern is consistent, but that doesn't mean it's consistently good! The Flatliner is an income investment, if it's an investment at all. It's certainly not for a growth investor such as you.

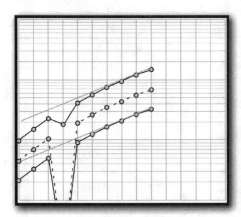

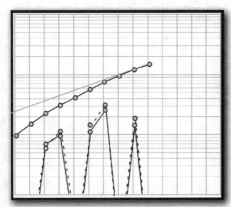

Figures 8.7. The Innocent Bystander   *Figure 8.8. Could Have Been a Contender*

The Innocent Bystander (Figure 8.7)

The *Innocent Bystander* is a company with an unblemished record, except that it had one bad year. Perhaps it had done too well before the apparent stumble. The company may have failed to write off everything it should have and then decided to take the hit that year and to do it right from then on. Usually a stumble such as this results from an accounting matter, although a hiccup in revenues such as the one that appears here could mean an internal problem in managing inventory or some other short-term, one-time issue that was resolved by a capable management team.

The performance during the bad year is data that you may eliminate as an outlier if you're satisfied that you fully understand what happened and feel it's safe to ignore it. A convenient rule of thumb is this: If eliminating the outlier decreases the slope of the trend line, then eliminate it. If eliminating the outlier increases the slope of the trend line, you should not eliminate the hiccup. You should wait until the bad year is far enough back in history to have little impact on the trend if eliminated. If the bad year occurred within the last four or five years, you should pass the company up and go on to another study. You can look at this company again in a year or two.

Could Have Been a Contender (Figure 8.8)

There's no question but that the *Could Have Been a Contender* company has had a fine record of sales growth, but its management has never been able to make money for its shareholders. This is better than your dot-com IPO that makes no money at all, but not by much.

Unless there's a good correlation between its top and bottom lines, a company such as this is iffy at best.

The Disaster (Figure 8.9)

A company with a chart similar to this is a *Disaster*. Need I say more? There's no point in continuing with a stock study when sales, earnings, or profits can't trudge uphill. A business doesn't have to look this bad to be an automatic discard, but when you see a bad one, you ought to be able to tell right away!

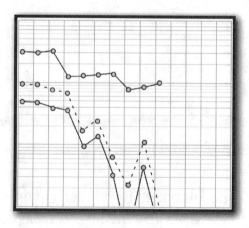

Figure 8.9. The Disaster

134

Some Real-World Examples

Let's look at some companies in the real world to see if you can put into practice what you've just finished reading. Look at each chart, consider how each compares with the pictures hanging in this "Gallery of Growth," and see if you draw the same conclusions I do.

In each case, I've included the data as well as the chart so that you can begin to get a feel for how data look when they're plotted.

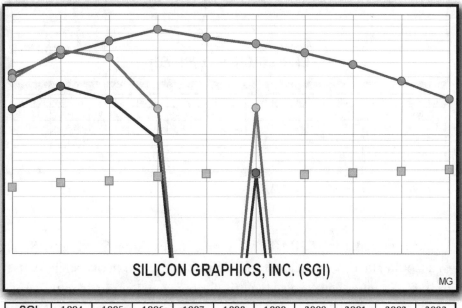

SILICON GRAPHICS, INC. (SGI)

MG

SGI	1994	1995	1996	1997	1998	1999	2000	2001	2002	2003
Sales	1537.8	2228.3	2921.3	3662.6	3100.6	2749.0	2331.1	1854.5	1341.4	961.7
Pre-tax	198.6	338.7	292.0	108.9	(391.4)	110.6	(279.0)	(364.1)	(37.8)	(125.9)
EPS	0.85	1.32	1.01	0.47	(1.46)	0.25	(3.96)	(2.06)	(0.01)	(0.50)
Shares	144.3	156.4	162.7	175.5	186.1	186.4	183.5	190.3	195.0	201.4

Figure 8.10. Silicon Graphics (SGI)

Silicon Graphics (SGI): Here's a company (see Figure 8.10) whose sales growth has obviously been declining seriously for the past six years. Earnings grew in 1995 but declined for the next two years, and, with the exception of 1999, the company lost money every year since. There's no point in bothering to continue with a study when sales and earnings are buried in the cellar as they are here. Companies in this condition are easy to spot. They are Disasters!

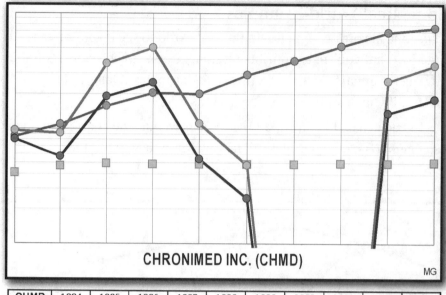

CHMD	1994	1995	1996	1997	1998	1999	2000	2001	2002	2003
Sales	49.0	62.5	90.5	117.2	115.6	168.6	222.5	297.9	397.4	435.7
Pre-tax	2.2	2.1	8.3	11.4	2.5	1.1	(3.8)	(7.0)	5.9	8.0
EPS	0.18	0.13	0.42	0.56	0.12	0.06	(0.03)	(0.37)	0.30	0.40
Shares	10.1	11.7	12.2	12.0	12.0	12.1	12.1	12.2	12.3	12.4

Figure 8.11. Chronimed, Inc. (CHMD)

Chronimed, Inc. (CHMD): Here's a good example (see Figure 8.11) of a Could Have Been a Contender. With the exception of a slight pause in 1998, revenues have grown beautifully; but what happened to the profits, the earnings, and the shareholders' interest in the company? Unless this company learns how to steady its expenses and to manage itself properly, it won't be a predictable and healthy company in which a shareholder would want to own a piece of the action.

NVR, Inc. (NVR): Here's an Arrowless Bow (see Figure 8.12). The growth rate of this homebuilder's revenues has been relatively steady at about 20 percent, a sustainable rate. But pre-tax profits and earnings are still growing at a much higher rate than sales even though their growth is declining steadily. The fact that pre-tax profit growth exceeds sales growth means that this company's management has been able to operate more and more efficiently, garnering an increasing number of pennies out of every dollar of sales each year.

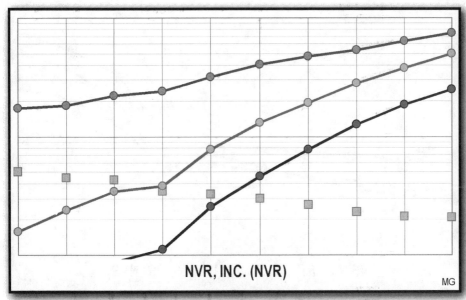

NVR, INC. (NVR)

MG

NVR	1994	1995	1996	1997	1998	1999	2000	2001	2002	2003
Sales	854.5	901.8	1076.7	1188.3	1559.8	2006.7	2316.4	2623.8	3136.3	3687.2
Pre-tax	22.2	33.4	48.7	53.9	110.4	185.2	272.6	394.7	536.0	704.7
EPS	0.53	1.07	1.70	2.18	4.97	9.01	15.30	24.86	36.05	48.99
Shares	17.1	15.3	14.6	11.8	11.1	10.2	9.1	7.9	7.3	7.1

Fig. 8.12 - NVR, Inc. (NVR)

The primary lesson to be learned here is that the growth of earnings has not yet stabilized. It continues to proceed at an unsustainable rate and therefore to decline. The fact that management has demonstrated its skill in improving profit margins would probably provide sufficient incentive to continue to pursue this study. You would probably estimate future growth within your comfort zone (see Chapter 10) and see where the rest of the analysis takes you.

New York Community Bancorp, Inc. (NYB): This is a company (see Figure 8.13) that has had a nice history of growth, suffered a slight decline in growth for one year, and then looks as if it was launched off a launch pad. The plotted data bounce up instead of down, and the "bowstring," were we to draw one, would be displayed across the top of the picture instead of the bottom. Here's your classic Rocket.

Typically, this kind of growth results primarily from acquisitions. There is little likelihood that any company could generate such acceleration in

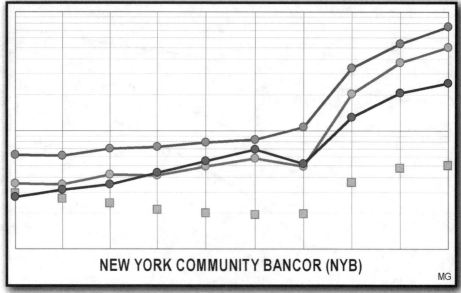

NYB	1994	1995	1996	1997	1998	1999	2000	2001	2002	2003
Sales	55.3	54.8	62.0	64.7	71.1	73.8	94.7	296.4	475.1	669.0
Pre-tax	32.3	31.9	38.7	37.6	45.1	52.4	45.4	183.7	336.0	455.1
EPS	0.17	0.19	0.21	0.27	0.33	0.42	0.32	0.79	1.25	1.52
Shares	111.3	100.1	92.8	81.8	76.3	74.1	75.4	136.4	180.9	189.8

Figure 8.13. New York Community Bancorp, Inc. (NYB)

revenues using only its own resources. And, in fact, this company participated in a "merger of equals" with another bank (Richmond County Financial) and became a holding company for the combined banks. This accounts for the immediate increase in revenues and also displays an increase in earnings, somewhat subdued by the increase in the number of shares outstanding as a result of the merger.

In the case of most acquisitions, adding the top line of the newly acquired companies to an already healthy top line can really paint a pretty picture. Note that earnings usually grow at a substantially lower rate than sales because extensive acquisition activity is most often accomplished by issuing new shares that dilute the earnings per share.

With a company such as this you should exercise caution because this kind of growth can't go on forever, and acquired companies often represent acquired problems.

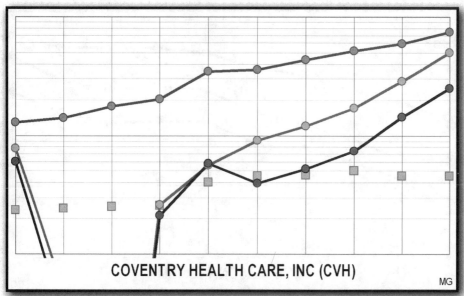

COVENTRY HEALTH CARE, INC (CVH)

MG

CVH	1994	1995	1996	1997	1998	1999	2000	2001	2002	2003
Sales	776.6	852.4	1057.1	1228.4	2110.4	2162.4	2604.9	3147.2	3576.9	4535.1
Pre-tax	60.7	3.8	(74.4)	20.3	44.0	71.7	93.6	134.7	225.7	393.1
EPS	0.66	0.03	(1.05)	0.23	0.63	0.44	0.57	0.82	1.59	2.76
Shares	45.8	47.3	49.2	49.8	78.7	88.5	89.3	97.5	88.8	88.1

Figure 8.14. Coventry Health Care, Inc. (CVH)

Coventry Health Care, Inc. (CVH): You're on your own here. Do you think Coventry (see Figure 8.14) would be a good buy?

This Innocent Bystander is a reasonably good prospect. It has had two bad years in its history—three if you count the year its earnings declined (1999). However, it's had a good track record since, has acquired additional companies along the way, and has been consistently good at converting revenues to profit, as you can see by the excellent growth of its pre-tax profit.

Legg Mason, Inc. (LM): Figure 8.15 looks to be a Motorcycle-type company. The telltale undulation in its revenue line is the distinguishing feature. Legg Mason's revenues appear to go up and down with the economic cycle; when they come back up, they exceed the revenues of the previous cycle. This is consistent with the type of business they're in: providing investment advice to entities and high-income individuals. It is this growth, and not the recent growth nor the earlier growth of profit

139

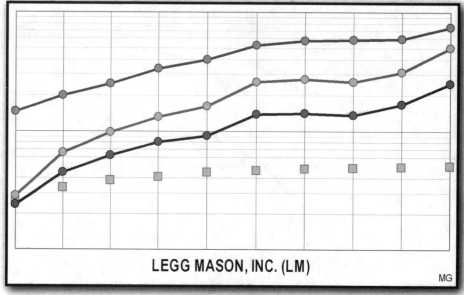

LM	1995	1996	1997	1998	1999	2000	2001	2002	2003	2004
Sales	389.1	533.3	664.6	889.1	1070.7	1399.6	1536.3	1548.9	1586.3	2004.3
Pre-tax	27.7	64.6	96.2	128.4	156.8	254.4	265.8	251.1	306.9	489.8
EPS	0.39	0.73	1.02	1.31	1.49	2.27	2.30	2.22	2.76	4.11
Shares	36.9	44.3	51.1	54.4	59.5	61.9	63.8	65.2	66.0	66.9

Figure 8.15. Legg Mason (LM)

and earnings, that you should consider if you're going to make this company a candidate. You will want to check the trend of growth between the highest points as revenues and earnings cycle.

You should now be in a good position to decide at first glance whether a company you're looking at is worthy of continued interest.

On the CD that accompanies this book, you'll find more companies whose data you can import into the technamental worksheet to try out your new skills.

The companies have been selected because they illustrate the points I've covered, and they offer you the opportunity for some good practice.

**Let's Take
Stock of**

What You Know About Identifying
Growth Patterns at a Glance

➤ As a company passes through its life cycle, its success and its potential as an investment can be sized up at a glance.

➤ Companies that are good candidates are easy to spot.

➤ More important, companies that are not good candidates are even easier to spot.

➤ As you become more experienced, you'll be able to gain more insight into what's in store for a company and why—just by glancing at its growth chart.

CHAPTER 9

Management's "Report Card"

If your candidate meets your growth requirements, the next step is to look at its efficiency and effectiveness. The fact that a company has exhibited the desired qualities in the past is no guarantee that it will continue to do so in the future. So you're interested in looking for signs that the future might be less rosy than the past.

Management has only two resources with which to generate earnings: revenue that comes in during the reporting period, and the equity of the company, which includes both the money that was paid by investors for stock issued and earnings retained from prior periods. As a beginning investor, you will be interested only in revenue. Equity can be an interesting and instructive measure under some circumstances, but, in my opinion, it should be accorded no more weight on management's report card than social skills should be given on a kid's. I'll discuss equity later in Chapter 13.

Profit Margins

To analyze the efficiency with which management uses the money it receives from the sale of goods or services, you will look at the return it earns on sales—the company's *profit margins*. Technamental investors like to look at the profit before taxes because management has no control over taxes.

143

The profit margin—the percent of revenue that remains as pretax profit after expenses have been paid—is calculated simply by dividing pretax profit by sales.

So if a company sold $100 million worth of goods or services and spent $90 million on various expenses excluding taxes, the remaining $10 million in pretax profit would represent a profit margin of 10 percent.

$100 (Sales) – $90 (Expenses) = $10 (Profit)

$10 (Profit) ÷ 100 (Sales) = 10% (Profit margin)

The higher that percentage figure, the more efficiently management has utilized the company's income. Trends in profit margins from year to year are an excellent indication of how capable and efficient management is—or isn't.

ABC Company, a nationally known producer of widgets and blivets, is fortunate. For every dollar it brings in, it makes an average of nearly 30 cents in profit before taxes. However, the percentages themselves are important only when you compare ABC Company with its peers in the same or similar industries. They are not nearly as important as the trend.

At one extreme, a food vendor is considered to be doing beautifully if it turns in a 4-percent profit margin. Because the grocery business relies on very high volume and very low markups of its products, the median profit margin in that industry is scarcely 2 percent.

On the other hand, a 25-percent profit margin in the computer software business would be very disappointing. The cost of hiring and retaining smart people is high, but much of the cost of developing new software products is incurred before a new product reaches the market. The actual expenses associated with the distribution of software products are relatively low. Companies whose products are intellectual and those whose products are tangible are not comparable.

There are two issues concerning profit margins that should take priority above all else. The first and by far more important item is the trend. The second item is stability.

If profit margins decline over a period of time, it's usually evidence that management is not doing as good a job of minding the store as it should. Costs are climbing and management is not doing what needs to be done to keep them under control.

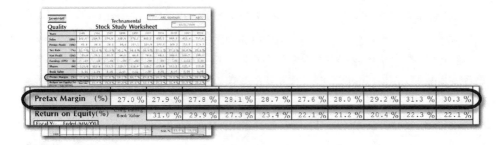

| Pretax Margin (%) | 27.0 % | 27.9 % | 27.8 % | 28.1 % | 28.7 % | 27.6 % | 28.0 % | 29.2 % | 31.3 % | 30.3 % |
| Return on Equity(%) | 31.0 % | 29.9 % | 27.3 % | 23.4 % | 22.1 % | 21.2 % | 20.4 % | 22.3 % | 22.1 % | |

Figure 9.1. ABC Company's Profit Margins

You can often analyze a trend quite easily just by looking at the figures. (See Figure 9.1.) You are particularly interested in margins for the most recent year or two, and you can compare them with the average for the last five years or so. If the most recent year's margin is higher than the five-year average, NAIC investors call it an uptrend. If the margin is no more than one-half a percent below the five-year average, then everything's probably okay.

As a technamental analyst, you may wish to plot the profit margins on a linear graph so you can see the trend clearly. (See Figure 9.2.)

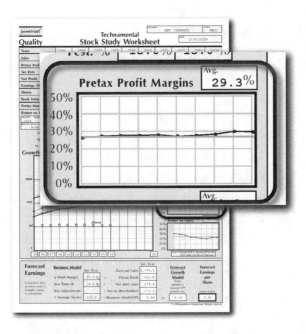

Figure 9.2. Linear Graph of Profit Margins for ABC Company

As you can see, ABC Company's profit margins have been pretty steady and have been trending slightly up. Drawing—or simply visualizing—a line that represents the average pretax profit margin makes it easy to see where the margins have been going.

Buying a company jet or building a palace to house the corporate headquarters are examples of decisions that can erode profit margins over time. Some such decisions may actually improve efficiency or are otherwise beneficial in the long run, but the results of bad decisions will eventually show up in the profit margins—and when they do, it's not very pretty.

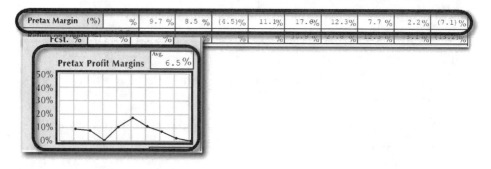

Pretax Margin	(%)		%	9.7 %	8.5 %	(4.5)%	11.1%	17.0%	12.3%	7.7 %	2.2%	(7.1)%

Figure 9.3. Declining Profit Margins at Midas, Inc.

Figure 9.3 displays 10 years of profit margins for Midas, Inc. (MDS). You don't need a chart to see the trend.

Midas is a well-known retail provider of automobile services that started out as the familiar Midas Muffler and extended its product line to other services and its scope into the international market place. Pretax margins in this industry are normally around 15 percent but, as you can see from the decline in the percentages, management at Midas appears to have taken a turn for the worse beginning about four years ago. The margins have declined each of the past four years and the company lost more than seven cents for each dollar of revenues in the last year. Needless to say, you would want to abandon your study of this company (if, in fact, you had even gone this far).

A flat trend is as good as an uptrend. If a company is operating as efficiently as it can, matching or bettering its peers in the profit margin department, then any attempts to cut costs could be counterproductive.

On the other hand, a company that's improving its margins must have had something to improve. So although its efforts are certainly commendable and appropriate, the company with an uptrend is not necessarily better than another company that's already operating at close to maximum efficiency.

After you have become more experienced, there will be times when a little research will lead you to excuse a minor or temporary downtrend. But as a new investor you should never consider investing in a company whose profit margins are declining.

The Real World

With more than 10,000 publicly traded companies out there to pick from, only a small minority will be suitable as long-term investments. This means, of course, that unless you take some pains to screen for companies that meet your requirements or find a source of suggestions such as the Roster of Quality Companies on the ICLUBcentral site (*www.iclub.com/support*), the great majority of companies you investigate will be unsuitable.

If you don't realize this up front and accept discouragement as a normal part of the process, you may tire of discarding company after company and give up. Worse yet, you may relax your requirements and accept companies that don't come up to snuff. Either way, you'll lose.

Remember: You need to own only about 10 to 20 good stocks—that's all! And there are plenty of companies to choose from to populate your portfolio. So be patient and disciplined.

To make you feel a little better about the prospects, I've listed 48 companies that appear to have met our quality standards for at least the five years prior to this writing. A strong disclaimer: Don't buy any of these companies unless you are certain they meet your own standards for quality and price.

More than one of these companies is likely to have suffered a setback since reporting the data I used. And even if performance on our quality criteria has persisted—as I'm sure it has for most—you'll find the price for many of these stocks unattractive. When I assembled this list, I made no effort to assess the price, just the quality.

ACS	Affiliated Computer Services	CBH	Commerce Bancorp, Inc.
APOL	Apollo Group	COCO	Corinthian Colleges, Inc.
AJG	Arthur J. Gallagher & Co.	EXBD	Corrporate Executive Board Co.
AXP	Axcan Pharma	CVH	Coventry Health Care
BLL	Ball Corporation		
OZRK	Bank of the Ozarks	DHI	D. R. Horton, Inc.
BZH	Beazer Homes USA	EBAY	EBay, Inc.
BBBY	Bed Bath and Beyond	EDMC	Education Management Corp.
BMET	Biomet	EASI	Engineered Support System
BFAM	Bright Horizons Family Solutions	FSH	Fisher Scientific International, Inc.
BRO	Brown & Brown, Inc.	FRX	Forest Labs
CAI	CACI International	GDW	Golden West Financial Corp.
CTX	Centex Corporaiton	HMA	Health Management Associates
CAKE	The Cheesecake Factory		
CHS	Chico's	HIBB	Hibbett Sporting Goods
CTSH	Cognizant Technology Solutions	HCG	Home Capital Group, Inc.

HOTT	Hot Topic, Inc.		LOW	Lowes Companies
HNP	Huaneng Power International		MDT	Medtronic, Inc.
			NVR	NVR Inc.
INFY	Infosys Technologies Limited		ORLY	O'Reilly Automotive, Inc.
IGT	International Game Technology		PDCO	Patterson Companies, Inc.
ESI	ITT Educational Services		PHM	Pulte Homes, Inc.
			RYAAY	Ryanair Holdings
KNGT	Knight Transportation		POOL	SCP Pool Corporation
LLL	L-3 Communications Holdings		SBUX	Starbucks Corporation
LNCR	Lincare Holdings, Inc.		WTFC	Wintrust Financial Corp.

Some of these companies have been around a long time and are familiar to you; others are not so well known. But all have been publicly traded for at least five years on the major exchanges and all have revenues of more than $100 million.

Figure 9.4 on pages 150–151 shows a chart for each of the companies so you can see what they have in common.

The moral of the story here is that you should keep the faith. There are plenty of fish in the sea for you, even though the sea is enormous and there are many more losers than winners.

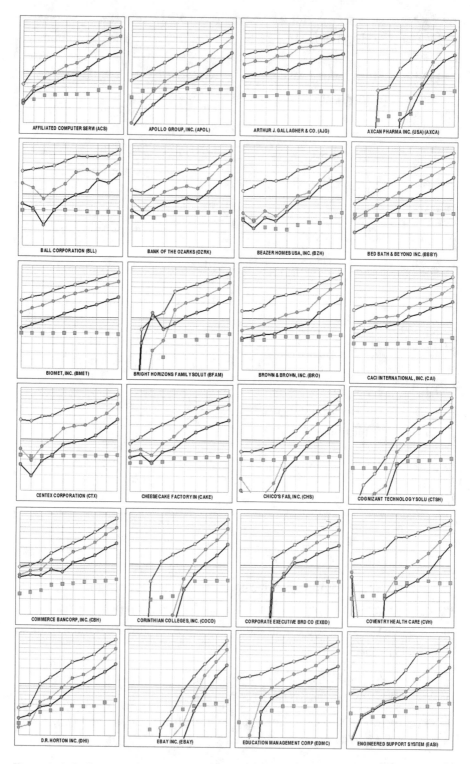

Figure 9.4. Gallery of Quality Companies (Part 1)

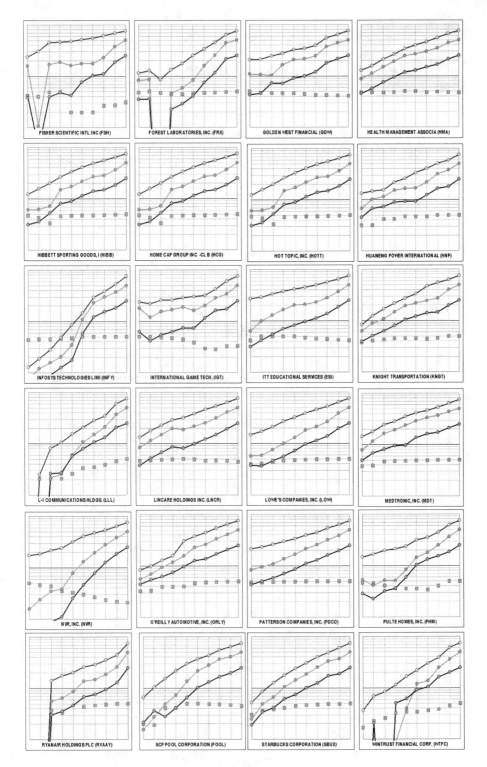

Figure 9.4. Gallery of Quality Companies (Part 2)

151

Let's Take Stock of | What You Know About Evaluating a Company's Quality

The two tests for quality that must be met are:

1. *Growth*. Sales and earnings growth must be strong enough to double your money every five years and stable enough to be predictable.

2. *Efficiency*. Profit margins must be stable, strong for their industry, and not declining.

You can tell if a company meets these requirements at a glance if you have the data and the technamental charts in hand. Nothing more is involved than making sure that the lines representing sales and earnings growth and profit margins are reasonably straight and are not sloping down.

Caution! If you compromise on quality, you can be seduced by the price. If in doubt, throw it out!

Your next step will be to find out whether the price is right and, if not, what the price ought to be.

CHAPTER 10

Evaluating the Price

You've completed the most important job: assessing a company's quality. Hopefully you won't have to find out the hard way that buying a good company for too high a price is still better than buying a poor company—even at what you may think is a bargain price. No matter how low it may be, a company that doesn't meet the quality requirements will always be too expensive—at any price!

Imagine a barbed-wire fence that stands between the quality issues that we have dealt with up until now and the value assessment we're about ready to embark on. If you're not critical enough about quality, you can easily be seduced into believing that a stock is a bargain when you actually shouldn't touch it with a 10-foot pole. So I want to paint as graphic a picture as I can to help you appreciate the consequence of trying to assess the value if you haven't paid enough attention to the quality.

Here's a statement that you may have to think about a little: *The worse a company performs, the better a value it will appear to be*. Why do you suppose that is?

If a company is performing badly, perhaps because management is not doing a good enough job of minding the store, and sales and earnings growth has decayed or declined, what will happen to the price? More people will want to sell than buy, and the price will go down, making the stock appear to be very cheap.

If you ignore the poor operational performance and just look at the price, you'll be in the market for someone else's mistake! Sure, you'll be able to pick up the stock at bargain-basement prices—but for a good reason. All of the benchmarks of a fair price that you're going to learn about in this chapter will look especially good. You'll think you made out like a bandit when, in fact, whomever you bought the stock from will turn out to be the lucky one.

The most important point here is that you simply can't afford to ignore the quality issues or treat them lightly. Unless the company completely satisfies your quality requirements—and I don't mean it's marginal or *might* have some problem—your evaluation of the price of the stock can be invalid and, in fact, hazardous to your financial health.

When in doubt, throw it out!

Fortunately, there are a couple of alarms that will go off if you bound over that barbed-wire fence recklessly or unawares. They're called the *historical value ratio* and the *risk index*, which we'll talk about in a little while.

The Process: An Overview

So you're now satisfied that a company is of sufficiently good quality to merit your continuing with the price evaluation. How do you know what that price should be? As was the case with the other steps you've learned so far, this process is very simple when you take it one step at a time.

As a long-term investor, your goal is to build a portfolio that will require little attention but will grow consistently in value over time, hopefully doubling every five years. To do this, you will need to think long term and push your horizon out at least five years into the future. That perspective allows you to eliminate the noise and clutter of the short-term stock market and focus on the underlying driver of a stock's price—the potential growth of earnings.

Let's pause just a moment to fully appreciate this change in perspective. Figure 10.1 on page 156 shows the price activity for Bed Bath & Beyond (BBBY) during the period from July 1, 1999 through June 30, 2000. The vertical bars represent the price activity during each week of the year, with the top of the bar representing the highest price that week, the bottom, the lowest, and the little crossbar the price when the market closed at the end of that week. The first thing that must strike you is that there is a lot of activity. In fact, during the course of any year, the price of any stock can fluctuate as much as 50 percent above or below the average price for the year for any number of reasons. Here, we've shown the highs, lows, and closes for a week at a time. You can imagine how the trader must stew about those movements on a daily or even hourly basis!

Had you been remarkably clairvoyant and bought Bed Bath & Beyond at its lowest point in the year (at $11.00, sometime during the first week in January 2000) and, calling again on your psychic sorcery, were able to sell it at the year's high ($22.75, three weeks later), you would have made $11.75 on the investment, or a robust 107 percent! But, lacking those powers, what do you suppose your chances would have been of buying that stock at those times? Slim to none, of course. Unless you have such a gift, you're like the rest of us. Had you bought that stock when the year began and sold it at the end of the year, you would have, in fact, lost money. And, except for that dip and almost immediate jump in price, a purchase and subsequent sale at any other times during the year would likely have produced a very lackluster result. Those price movements simply cannot be predicted.

Let's take a different perspective, however, and step back far enough to look at a five-year period. The first thing you will notice in Figure 10.2 on page 156 is that the weekly ups and downs are no longer significant. They blend together to create a broad line that, although erratic, shows a definite uptrend over the five-year period. That's what I mean about causing the daily and weekly fluctuations to fade into insignificance. It's the long-term trend that is of much greater interest.

The little white lines plotted beneath the price line are the reported earnings per share. It's easy to see that the trend in prices over the long term parallels the trend in earnings. Hopefully, you'll learn to pay more attention to graphs displaying earnings than to those displaying prices by the time you finish this book. Earnings are far more predictable and, over the long haul, are what drive the price.

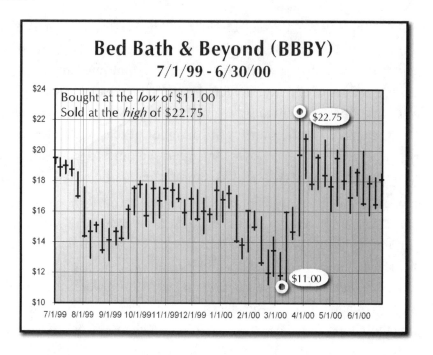

Figures 10.1. Bed Bath & Beyond (BBBY) One Year

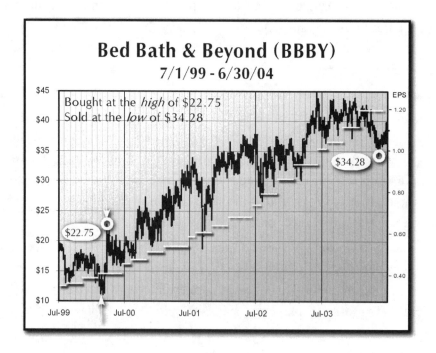

Figures 10.2. Bed Bath & Beyond (BBBY) Five Years

Note that you could have bought Bed Bath & Beyond *at its highest point during the year* ($22.75, in the fourth week in March 2000) and sold it at the worst possible time ($34.28, in the last week of November 2003), when it plummeted to its lowest point for more than a year, and still made more than 8.5 percent on your investment, compounded annually.

The point is that, when you invest in good quality companies for the long term, you don't need to worry all that much about whether you bought them at the lowest point or not. You can easily determine what a fair price would be and be confident that you're going to make money most of the time.

Had you bought Bed Bath & Beyond at its *average* price during the first year ($16.47) and sold it only at its average price five years later ($39.93) you would have made an excellent compounded return of nearly 20 percent—comfortably above what you're shooting for!

So let's look at how we would determine the fair price.

Return and Risk

When it comes to evaluating the price of a stock, you're really interested in just two things: the potential *return* and the *risk* you must take to get that return. If the potential return is worth the risk, the price is right. If it's not, you can simply wait until it is. As volatile as the stock market is, most stocks will sell at a favorable price sometime during the year.

In order to estimate the potential return, you'll have to come up with a reasonable forecast of how high the price might go. To do that you will draw upon history to estimate what earnings might be in five years and what multiple of those earnings you can expect investors to pay for the stock in the future. With those two estimates, you can readily calculate a hypothetical high price with which you can estimate the potential return.

To evaluate the risk, you'll repeat the process you went through to estimate the return, this time combining a low estimate for future earnings with the lowest multiple you might reasonably expect investors to pay. This will result in a conservative estimate of the stock's potential lowest price. If the *risk index* you calculate tells you that your potential gain is at least three times as much as you risk losing, your stock is probably selling at a fair price.

Again, there are some housekeeping chores that must be done to begin with. The computer does them nicely. If you're working manually, the chores are somewhat more tedious and time-consuming. But they're not all that complicated—especially with your financial calculator.

Estimating the Potential Return on Your Investment

Estimating the potential return on your investment requires four steps:

1. Estimating future PEs.

2. Estimating future earnings.

3. Using those values to estimate the potential high price.

4. Calculating the return should the price go up to that high price in the next five years.

The illustrations in this chapter and the next were produced with the automated worksheet on the CD in the back of this manual. If you haven't already done so, I suggest you take a few moments at this time to install the CD on your computer. Launch "Take Stock" and select the third option on the menu ("Analyze a Company"). Select "ABC Company" from the list and click on "Value." You can then follow along as we go through the steps ahead.

Estimating Future PEs

Your first step is to look at what multiples of earnings (PEs) investors have historically paid for the stock at various times, both when they were confident and optimistic about the company (producing the highest PE each year) and when they were the least confident (producing the lowest PE).

Eliminating PE outliers. Before you can draw any conclusions from those values, however, you will want to eliminate outliers—data that is historically irrelevant—just as you did when you analyzed growth. Outlandish PEs, of greatest significance when they are on the high side, are typically caused by one of two things: abnormally low earnings reported after the high price has been recorded for the year, or "irrational exuberance" on the part of investors who pay excessive prices not justified by the earnings.

158

If you're using a computer, the high and low multiples and the averages will have already been calculated for you. If you're doing this by hand, you will have completed those calculations when you prepared your worksheet.

Look for PEs that are out of line with the rest.

Value							Company ABC COMPANY			Ticker ABCC
Earnings	.27	.36	.46	.56	.61	.69	.82	.94	1.11	1.32
High Price	9.70	32.40	30.50	16.50	14.30	19.90	20.60	27.00	41.20	45.80
Low Price	4.90	8.10	13.80	8.40	9.00	13.10	12.50	14.30	23.60	24.60
High P/E	35.9	90.0	66.3	29.5	23.4	28.8	25.1	28.7	37.1	34.7
Low P/E	18.1	22.5	30.0	15.0	14.8	19.0	15.2	15.2	21.3	18.6
Average P/E	27.0	56.2	48.2	22.2	19.1	23.9	20.2	22.0	29.2	26.6
Dividends										
Years	1995	1996	1997	1998	1999	2000	2001	2002	2003	2004

Figure 10.3. ABC Company's Price, EPS, and PE History

The quickest way to find such offending PEs is to simply eyeball the high and low PEs, looking for those that are obviously out of whack. Look at ABC Company's PEs in Figure 10.3. It isn't difficult to pick out the ones that are out of line, is it? This case is pretty cut-and-dried. High PEs of 90.0 and 66.3 and low PEs of 22.5 and 30 in 1996 and 1997 are obviously way out of line with the rest. However, you may not get off so easy the next time, because PE outliers aren't always quite so obvious. And, just because a PE is high doesn't mean it's an outlier. In fact, many companies won't have any PEs that are out of line at all.

For the less-noticeable cases, plotting the PEs on a linear graph will help. In figure 10.4 on page 160, ABC Company's extraneous data hits you right between the eyes.

The dots in Figure 10.4 plot the high, low, and average PEs, and average PEs are connected to better show the trends. The upper and lower bands represent the average of the high and low PEs, respectively, and the band through the center represents the signature PE. The dotted lines have been included to show estimates of future high and low PEs, which we'll discuss shortly.

159

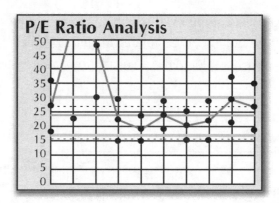

Figure 10.4. ABC Company: Linear Graph of PEs

Eliminating the outliers takes only a couple of mouse-clicks on the computer. If you're doing the study by hand, simply scratch out the offending numbers and calculate your averages for the high, low, and average PEs using the remaining data, as in Figure 10.3. I suggest that you strike out both the high and low PEs in any year in which either one appears excessive.

Some of the software products bypass the exercise of seeking and eliminating PE outliers and, instead, default to the *median* of all of the PE values to calculate the signature PE. This is a statistical method of determining the central tendency of a series of data that simply lines up all the data from the highest to the lowest and picks the one in the middle—or the average of the two in the middle if there are an even number of values. Thus the highest and lowest values, regardless of how far out of line they may be, don't influence the result.

The historical value ratio (HVR). Once you have averaged the remaining, *relevant* historical average multiples, you have what you need for a reality check on the current price. The historical value ratio (HVR) is a warning device that can tell you if you've missed something in your quality assessment.

In Chapter 4, I explained that the signature PE is the somewhat unique price-earnings ratio that is tied to a company. Over time a company consistently attracts investors at a certain multiple of earnings.

Depending on which industry the company is in and the company's particular niche in that industry, investors will confer upon it a certain confidence level. This translates into a PE multiple that stays with it, more or less, throughout its life. Barring any serious problems, that PE will persist, although it will typically display a slight decline as the company's growth slows with the company's continuing success and increasing size.

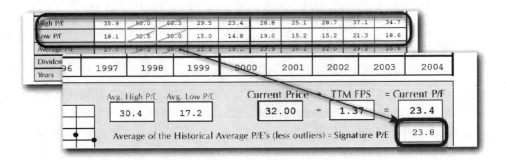

Figure 10.5. Calculating the Signature PE

Investors who buy stock in a company at a PE greater or less than its signature PE will find that the price tends to gravitate down or up toward that PE, and they will suffer or benefit accordingly.

To approximate the signature PE, remove the irrelevant historical data and average the remaining historical high and low PEs. (See Figure 10.5.) If you use a computer, there's no work to it; it's all done for you. If you're working by hand, don't be lazy! Calculate the average of the high, low, and average PEs from *all* of the years you have available (less the outliers, of course). The more data you use, the less effect variations will have on the average, and the more valid the signature PE will be. A large segment of the market has been overvalued during the recent bubble. Including the earlier PEs in the average can moderate the effect of those recent wilder times.

For ABC Company, with 1996 and 1997 removed, the 10-year average PE is about 23.8. (Had you not removed the outliers, the 10-year average would have been an exaggerated 29.5.) Now that you've come up with your signature PE, you can compare it with the current PE to see how today's price compares with the historically fair price of the stock (measured as a multiple of earnings). This comparison is the historical value ratio (HVR), which NAIC educators call *relative value*. I use *HVR* because *relative value* is confused with terms used in other quarters for other things and to distinguish it from NAIC's RV, which makes use of only five years of PE history. HVR and relative value are, however, identical in their purpose and use.

If you're using the computer, the HVR (or RV) is calculated for you. If you're doing the study by hand, you'll first have to calculate the current PE (the current price divided by the sum of the earnings for the most recent four quarters) and then divide the result by the signature PE. (See Figure 10.6.) The current PE for ABC Company is 23.4 (32 ÷ 1.37). When we divide this figure by the signature PE (23.8), we come up with an HVR (or relative value) of 98.3 percent. This means that the stock is currently selling for a multiple that's just a trifle under the historical average; the price is reasonable in view of the past.

In general, you are looking for an HVR of right around 100 percent or a bit less. Obviously, if you can buy a quality stock today for a historically fair price, you should probably do so, provided the next steps show the reward and risk to be attractive.

However, what should you do if you find that the HVR is significantly above or below the 100-percent mark?

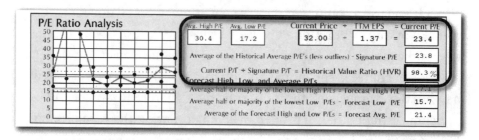

Figure 10.6. Calculating the Historical Value Ratio (HVR)

A low HVR is probably your biggest concern, because it suggests that people who are buying the stock today might know something negative about the company that you don't know.

Think about it. Why would investors pay less for the stock than it has typically sold for? Is there something in the news that you haven't heard about? Has an analyst—or have a number of analysts—announced a reduced expectation of future earnings based upon something they know that you don't know? Have you missed something in your quality analysis—or (shame on you!) recklessly jumped over that barbed-wire fence, failing to evaluate quality deliberately enough before moving on to look at the value considerations? My strong recommendation to new investors is to start off by simply disciplining themselves to be mechanical about it.

If the HVR is too low—below 85 percent—move on to another company and forget about looking at the risk and reward. You may miss a few good stocks, but you won't have to lose any sleep worrying about being wrong.

If the HVR is too high, above around 110 percent or so, this tells you two things. The first is that other investors appear to agree with you about the quality issues, because they are paying a healthy price for the stock. The second is that it may be too healthy a price. You may want to put off buying it until the price becomes more reasonable. Or, it may be worth the premium, if the risk and reward are satisfactory.

Just know that, if you buy a stock whose PE is too far above the signature PE, when it later comes back down—which it usually will—the decrease in PE can reduce your gain considerably. There's simply no need to take unnecessary risks, especially when you're starting out. Your chances of having a superior portfolio are far better if you select stocks for which you don't have to make any allowances.

As you gain more experience, you'll find that you can make some intelligent exceptions in cases of high or low HVR; but for now, don't.

Completing your PE estimates. The next step will be to make a reasonable and conservative estimate of future multiples, both high and low. Again, I suggest that you do this task mechanically to begin with. Later you may think about moderating your estimates, but not until you have the experience to come up with good reasons for doing so.

Your mechanical process is simply to average the lowest half or majority of your data. If you have 10 years of data, scratch out the highest five numbers and average the rest. If you have nine years of data, get rid of the highest four and average the remaining five, and so on. If you have only five years of data, you should average only the lowest three, and, if you have fewer than five years, *you ought to be looking at an older company*. In no case forecast a high PE of greater than 30.

For ABC Company, the maximum high and low PEs occurred from 1995 through 1997 and in 2003 and 2004. Eliminating those and averaging the remaining high PEs, you would come up with a forecast high PE of 27.1. Had the result been greater than 30, you would have limited it to 30. (Note: The figures with Xs through them in Figure 10.7 are the outliers. Those with a single diagonal line through them are eliminated to establish the forecast high and low PEs.) Using the same process, you find that the average of the five lowest low PEs is 15.7. This is the forecast low PE. The average of the forecast high PE (27.1) and the forecast low PE (15.7) is the forecast average PE: 21.4.

In many cases, the high numbers you delete for both the forecast high PE and the forecast low PE will occur in the same years. As in the case of ABC Company, however, this won't necessarily be the case every time. So you should examine and eliminate the high numbers for the forecast high PE and the forecast low PE independently.

Value							Company ABC COMPANY			Ticker ABCC
Earnings	.27	.36	.46	.56	.61	.69	.82	.94	1.11	1.32
High Price	9.70	32.40	30.50	16.50	14.30	19.90	20.60	27.00	41.20	45.80
Low Price	4.90	8.10	13.80	8.40	9.00	13.10	12.50	14.30	23.60	24.60
High P/E	35.9	90.0	66.3	29.5	23.4	28.8	25.1	28.7	37.1	34.7
Low P/E	18.1	22.5	30.0	15.0	14.8	19.0	15.2	15.2	21.3	18.6
Average P/E	27.0	55.2	48.2	22.2	19.1	23.9	20.2	22.0	29.2	26.6

For both the high and low P/Es: If you have nine or ten years of data, average the lowest five. If you have only seven or eight, average the lowest four. If you have just five or six, average the lowest three. If you have fewer than five years of data, wait until you do have at least five years of data.

Current P/E ÷ Signature P/E = Historical Value Ratio (HVR) | 98.3 %

Forecast High, Low, and Average P/Es

Average half or majority of the lowest High P/Es Forecast High P/E	27.1
Average half or majority of the lowest Low P/Es Forecast Low P/E	15.7
Average of the Forecast High and Low P/Es – Forecast Avg. P/E	21.4

Figure 10.7. Averaging the Lowest Half or Majority

A word of caution is in order here. In Chapter 6, I likened the life of a corporation to that of a human being. Many of the "hot" companies you'll be attracted to are still in a stage of "corporate adolescence." Be careful! They have not been seasoned as "adults" have. Many of them are the so-called new-economy businesses whose managements have not had to deal much with economic downsides.

Often the technology that such companies offer is unique. Their intellectual monopolies afford them the sort of protection that kids take for granted before they have to grapple with the cold, cruel world on their own. As do strapping high school football heroes, new-economy companies think they're ready to conquer the world, but they haven't yet experienced an economy without euphoria or a market with healthy competition.

Citrix Systems (CTXS) comes to mind as an example. Not three months before I wrote the first edition of this book, Citrix executives bragged that, of its 1,100 employees, more than 700 were millionaires! This was, of course, because their stock options looked fantastic on paper. From a high of around $122 at that time, the stock price plunged to around $20 on news of a disappointing quarter and went on to decline to less than $15. Citrix is an excellent company with great products and promises and a corps of smart employees and dedicated managers. But I'll wait to consider buying its stock until it has marshaled those resources and proved that it can survive its bump in the road. So far, it's been a struggle.

The point? Don't even consider a fairly new company with a history of rising PEs and no sign of a downturn. Where investor confidence has never been challenged, a past without problems is definitely not a harbinger of an untroubled future. Companies that have been consistently meeting analysts' extraordinary estimates from the day they first attracted attention are an investor's disaster waiting to happen—and perhaps an opportunity when it does.

Estimating Future Earnings

In order to estimate earnings five years into the future, you will need to estimate the rate at which earnings will grow for those five years. Chances are that, when you're looking at historical growth, you'll go on to forecast future growth.

It makes a lot of sense to use the historical information that you've developed while it's fresh. That's the way all of the software is structured, as are the worksheets for those who do their calculations by hand. For purposes of this book, however, I held off on the discussion of forecasting until now rather than muddying the waters with value issues as we talked about quality.

165

Except in very rare cases, companies can't sustain extremely strong growth rates forever. A company's success alone is enough to work against the perpetuation of high rates. The bigger a company gets, the greater the level of sales and earnings it has to generate in order to keep up its rate of growth.

The first thing to recognize, therefore, is that growth rates of even the greatest companies will eventually decline. It's a fact of life. If you're estimating growth for the long term—not just for the next year—it's very likely that the historical growth rate of both sales and earnings will decline at least a little.

The next consideration when forecasting growth is predictability—the stability of past growth. If the lines that connect the annual dots are smooth on your growth chart, it's relatively easy to forecast growth rationally. As I've noted, you're much more likely to see smooth historical growth lines on the chart for sales than for earnings because sales are influenced by far fewer things than are earnings. Therefore, you're going to have more confidence in your estimates of sales growth than in your estimates of earnings growth. You will estimate future sales growth at a rate closer to the historical sales growth rate than you will future earnings growth relative to the historical earnings growth rate.

Your aim is to produce estimates of future growth rates for sales and earnings that you feel comfortable with and that you believe are sustainable—not only for the next five years, but for the next 20 or more.

Some limiting rules of thumb. Here are a couple of general rules of thumb that will keep you inside the ballpark and out of trouble.

First, let sales be your guide. Because sales are more stable and are therefore more predictable, estimate sales growth first. Then, never estimate future earnings growth at a rate higher than that of sales. Earnings growth depends upon the rate of sales growth; differences between the two growth rates are only transient. Earnings growth at a rate faster than that of sales growth is simply not sustainable. Period.

Second, establish a sensible cap on growth estimates. Make it a hard and fast rule to *never predict future sales or earnings to grow at a rate greater than 20 percent.*

Even 20 percent is rarely sustainable for very long, although in recent years a number of companies have demonstrated remarkable staying power at and above that rate and have held those high rates for more years than anyone could have imagined possible.

One case in point has been the pharmaceutical industry. Many drug companies have discovered a formula for growing earnings that seems as elusive and incredible as perpetual motion. Using a combination of tax write-offs for research and development costs and the perpetual increase in the prices of patent-protected products, many drug companies have found a way to grow their earnings at a rate faster than sales growth—for decades. However, don't gamble that you may be the clever one to have found the next company or industry to perform the same feat. The odds are definitely against it.

Remember: Your aim is to find companies that can provide you with a return of 15 percent or better. If you can't get that kind of return from investing in a company with 20 percent earnings growth, there's probably something wrong with the investment anyway! I would hate to have to rely upon any growth above 20 percent to produce my desired return. (Of course, any excess *beyond* my expectations would be gratefully accepted!) With these constraints in mind, here are the commonsense considerations you'll take into account as you forecast the future.

Forecasting sales growth. If sales growth has described a perfectly straight line on the growth chart for all of the years that are plotted, it's easy to figure out what the future probably holds. You can feel comfortable estimating that future sales will grow at a rate close to, but a little below, their historical rate. In fact, you might consider rounding the historical rate down to the next lower whole percentage and let it go at that. Bed Bath & Beyond (BBBY) is a good example of a company with a stable but slowing growth rate. (See Figure 10.8.) However, lines are rarely perfectly straight. If the line has a sawtooth pattern or zigzags as it climbs across the chart as with Quadrax (QDXC), sales growth is not predictable. Therefore, you can't depend upon steady growth in the future. This is more likely to be the case for earnings than for sales, but occasionally both lines exhibit the zigzag pattern.

A company with a zigzag pattern may have attracted your interest because of its comfortable uptrend. However, the more erratic the growth line appears to be, the greater the allowances you have to make for disappointment. It's best you discard any company whose historical growth has meandered too much for you to be comfortable with a forecast.

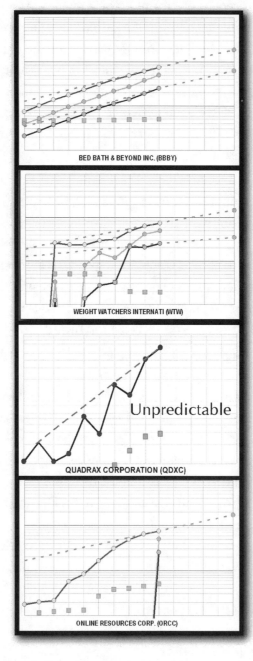

Figure 10.8. Variations in Sales Growth

Be careful of younger companies. They will usually show rapid growth rates, then rapid decay. Be sure to take into account the decay as you project the growth into the future.

Forecasting earnings growth. The principle for estimating earnings growth is the same as that for sales, but earnings are apt to be less predictable. Because earnings are derived from sales, whatever volatility sales display, earnings will most likely mirror. Compounding that volatility are all of the fluctuations in expenses, taxes, and the number of shares outstanding that come into play before you finally get to the bottom line.

To estimate the growth rate of earnings, use the relevant historical growth rate as a starting point and temper it with enough conservatism to make you comfortable, being certain that your estimate doesn't exceed your estimate of sales growth.

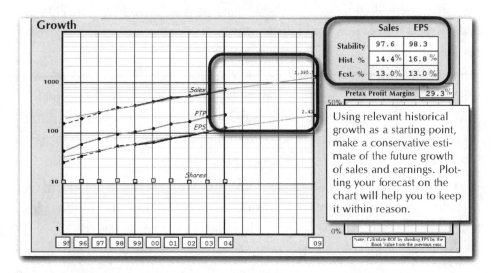

Figure 10.9. ABC Company's Growth Forecast

For ABC Company, after the outliers were eliminated, the historical sales growth rate came out at around 14 percent, earnings at nearly 17 percent (the computer came up with 14.4 and 16.8 percent, respectively). Just to be especially conservative, I've chosen to estimate sales growth in the future at only 13 percent and, of course, earnings at a figure that is no higher despite past rapid earnings growth.

Now you can estimate what sales and earnings will be in five years. On the computer you will simply enter your estimated growth rates for sales

169

and earnings into the appropriate fields, and the computer will draw your trend lines out five years, calculating the sales and earnings at that point.

If you're working by hand, you'll use your business calculator to enter the data. Put in your sales information first, using last fiscal year's data as the present value:

PV = 757.4

N = 5 (years)

i% = 13

Solve for FV, the future value of sales.

You'll plot the result (1,395.5) on the right margin. Next, you have only to replace the sales figure with the earnings figure (1.32) as the PV and, because the growth rate is the same, you're ready to solve for FV again. You will come up with 2.43, which you can also plot. You'll then draw your lines from the data for the most recent year to these newly plotted points.

The Business Model: another view of future earnings. There are two approaches you can use to estimate future earnings. The first, which I just described, requires you to conservatively estimate future earnings growth and then calculate what earnings would be five years out, if they were to grow at that rate. The second approach is the *business model*.

Used together, these approaches offer two dissimilar perspectives, each helping to corroborate the result—a sort of "financial depth perception" that can give you a more realistic view.

Users of the business model attempt to track the company's future income as it runs the gauntlet from the top to the bottom line—just as a company operates. NAIC investors familiar with this approach call it the *preferred procedure*.

In the first edition of this book, I included this information in Chapter 14, "Finer Points and Fudge Factors," because I thought it to be an advanced concept that might confuse a new investor. At that time I urged readers to forego using this device until they were completely comfortable with the first method of forecasting earnings. I've since changed my mind.

Now, I strongly recommend that you go ahead and use it. It's an excellent way to understand how a business operates and to grasp the relationships among the elements that contribute to the company's earnings per share. And, it can give you more confidence in the value you finally decide on for future earnings. We'll use ABC Company's figures for our example. (See Figure 10.10.)

Pretax Profit (\$M)	43.8	58.0	70.5	94.4	107.1	124.9	149.0	169.5	205.8	229.7
Tax Rate (%)	31.7%	32.6%	32.3%	32.2%	34.8%	36.6%	37.1%	37.1%	38.8%	35.1%
Net Profit (\$M)	29.9	39.5	51.8	64.0	69.8	79.2	94.1	106.5	124.7	149.1
Earnings (EPS) (\$)	.27	.36	.46	.56	.61	.69	.82	.94	1.11	1.32
Shares (M)	110.4	112.4	113.5	115.3	114.4	115.2	115.8	111.2	112.0	112.6
Book Value	1.16	1.54	2.05	2.61	3.12	3.86	4.61	4.97	5.96	6.89
Pretax Margin (%)	27.0%	27.9%	27.8%	28.1%	28.7%	27.6%	28.0%	29.2%	31.3%	30.3%

Forecast Earnings	**Business Model**	5yr. Fcst.		5yr. Fcst.	**Forecast Growth Model**	**Forecast Earnings per Share**
				Forecast Sales 1,395.5		
	x Profit Margin	30.0%	=	Pretax Profit 418.6	From growth at forecast EPS	
Complete this section only if Growth, above, is satisfactory	less Taxes @	35.1%	=	Net after taxes 271.7	growth rate.	Lower of two
	less Adjustments	−		Net to shareholders 271.7		
	÷ Average Shares	113.0	=	Business Model EPS **2.40** or	**2.43** =	**2.40**

© 2000 Inve\$tWare Corporation. All rights reserved.

Figure 10.10. Applying the Business Model to Estimate Future Earnings

Because a company's sales are impacted by far fewer factors and are therefore more stable, you can have greater confidence in your forecast of sales than of earnings. So we start with sales. The business model begins with default values for each of the major elements of a company's income statement—values that you will use unless you have a compelling reason to change them.

1. **Forecast sales.** At our forecast growth rate of 13 percent, ABC Company should produce \$1,395.5 million in sales in fiscal 2004. This is our starting point.

2. **Profit.** The next step is to estimate how much of that revenue will be left after expenses are paid. Because the profit margin represents the percentage of sales that remain after expenses are paid, we look at the profit margin. The default value is the average profit margin we've already calculated for the past five years.

   Here's where your technamental analysis can prove very helpful. Look at the annual profit margins—or the chart on which they are plotted. (Refer to Figures 9.1 and 9.2 in Chapter 9.)

171

ABC Company has done a great job of tightening up its costs, causing the profit margins to trend up. When you look at a company whose margins have stabilized at a higher rate in the most recent years, you might consider raising your estimated future margin some to reflect that improvement. ABC Company has achieved margins in excess of 30 percent for the last couple of years. So it would be reasonable to round this figure off at 30 percent as an estimate for the future. When we multiply the sales figure by margin, we arrive at a *pretax profit* of $418.6 million. Of course, if the margin had been declining, you probably would have already rejected the study for that reason.

3. **Taxes.** The next thing a business does is to pay taxes on its pretax profit. The default value for taxes is the amount of the taxes of the prior year. Unless you have reason to believe that Uncle Sam or his chums in the state capitals are going to make a serious change in the tax rates within the next five years, you can use the default value for taxes. Some like to use Value Line's estimate for future taxes in this field.

Looking at the annual tax rates, we will stay with 35.1 percent from last year. So let's deduct 35.1 percent of the pretax profit, or $146.9 million, leaving a *net after taxes* of $271.7 million from which to deduct any further adjustments before allocating the remainder to the shares.

4. **Adjustments to income.** This is a catchall that allows you to include any items you can think of that might affect the bottom line after taxes. The adjustment most frequently found would be preferred dividends. For companies that are paying preferred shareholders, their dividends are the most predictable such charge and would be the default value.

If you are using your computer, you can look at the income statement for whatever company you are studying on the Reuters site (*www.investor.reuters.com*). This is probably the best "one-stop shopping" site for information about a company that's available. You must register but, at this writing, it's free.

ABC Company has no preferred shareholders so the *net available to common shares* is still $274.4 million.

5. **Shares outstanding.** You should estimate the number of shares that will be outstanding five years in the future. The default value is the current number of shares.

   Look at the last 10 years for common shares outstanding, which you'll find in the data section of your computer program or on the worksheet. Has the company had a history of issuing shares on a regular basis and increasing its capitalization that way? Has your research revealed that the company has embarked on a share repurchase program, which tends to reduce the number of shares? You can look at Value Line's estimate (in the right column) or simply add more shares based on the company's history. (Don't reduce the number of shares, because that would give you a less conservative earnings figure when you're finished.)

   I chose to round off the number of shares to an even 113.0, just to be a little more conservative.

6. **Earnings per share.** When you divide the net available to common shares by the forecast number of shares, you'll come up with an estimate of future earnings per share (EPS) using the business model. ABC Company would be expected to produce $271.7 ÷ 113, or *$2.40, earnings per share*.

   As you can see, this estimate is almost the same as what you calculated by simply extrapolating earnings growth. And this is the purpose of this exercise: to compare the result from the business model with the result arrived at using the basic method.

   Use the lower of the two results as I have in this example—especially if there is a substantial difference between them.

Estimating the Potential High Price

Your next task is to figure out what the potential high price will be if earnings grow as you forecast and the PE meets your conservative expectation.

It's simple. Multiply your forecast earnings by the multiple of those earnings you expect investors to pay (your forecast high PE), and you'll arrive at the highest potential high price you might expect.

We forecast that ABC Company can produce $2.40 per share in earnings in the year ending in May of 2009, and its stock could sell at a high multiple of 27.1 times those earnings. The product of the two figures is $65.04—the potential high price. That's simple enough, isn't it?

Calculating the Return

Your *return* is the hypothetical profit you will make if you buy a stock at today's price and sell it in five years at its potential high price, receiving any dividends the company might pay over that time. Return is expressed as a *compounded, annualized* percentage.

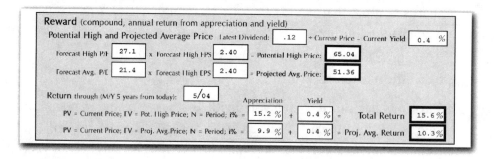

Figure 10.11. Calculating the Total Return and the Average Return for ABC Company

As you can see, return has two components: *appreciation* (growth of the original investment), which is of primary interest to you as an investor in growth companies, and *yield* (the dividend income that you might receive along the way).

Now we need to figure out the compounded annual return. Again, the computer does the job handily so that all you have to do is read the return off the screen. If you're working manually, finding the return is just a matter of plugging the data into your calculator and reading the result.

PV = the current price ($32.00)

FV = your forecast high price ($65.04)

N = the number of years in the future for which you're projecting—usually five

Solve for i%, the compounded annual appreciation.

In this case, your investment in ABC Company would hypothetically appreciate 15.2 percent each year for the next five.

This is a simple enough result and you might well let it go at that. However, if you are a stickler for detail and wish to add a little complexity in the interest of being more "accurate"—an interesting word when we're merely coming up with hypothetical forecasts—we can go a step further. (Don't feel obliged to, but it's something to consider as you progress.)

This result overlooks the fact that today, the day of the study, is well past the end of the last full fiscal year. In fact, our example is a full six months after the last fiscal year ended and earnings have already been reported for the first quarter of the new fiscal year. So, you might wish to account for the fact that, five years from today's date, earnings will have grown larger than your projected earnings—having grown for another quarter, and the price will have had six more months to reach the high price calculated using those additional earnings.

In order to compensate for this discrepancy, we will need to grow earnings for another quarter to calculate the high price. There are two possible scenarios for this: Extend the period of earnings growth for the additional number of quarters, or grow the sum of the trailing four quarters' earnings for a full five years. We can then use the more conservative of the two results to calculate our high price and total return. Let's see how that would work in the case of ABC Company.

Option 1, using last year's earnings:

PV = earnings for the last full fiscal year ($1.32)

i% = your selected earnings growth rate (13)

N = 5.25 years, to account for the additional quarter's growth

Solving for FV, the result would be $2.51.

Option 2, using the trailing 12 months' earnings:

PV = total earnings for the last four quarters ($1.37; see Figure 7.11 in Chapter 7)

i% = your selected earnings growth rate (13)

N = 5 years

Solving for FV, the result would be $2.52.

Using the lesser of the two results and multiplying that value ($2.51) times the forecast high PE (27.1), we arrive at a potential high price five years from *today* of $68.02.

Next, to calculate the new value for appreciation:

PV = the current price ($32)

FV = the new figure for the forecast high price ($68.02)

N = 5 years

Solving for i%, the result is a value for appreciation of 16.3 percent.

This is a substantial increase over the original calculation of 15.2 percent and appears to be worth the extra effort. Needless to say, variations in the number of quarters and estimated growth rates will produce results of greater or lesser consequence. But, it's my opinion that it's going to be worth the extra effort, after you have had the chance to get comfortable with the simple method.

Yield. You're a growth company investor, so yield won't have much of an impact on your investment return. In fact, you're mostly interested in the companies whose policymakers feel that they can best increase shareholder value by plowing earnings back into their own operations to feed their growth.

Yield is nevertheless a part of your return, and, if you're investing in a General Electric (GE) or some other large, established company to balance your risk and anchor your portfolio, you're definitely going to need to factor it in.

The simplest way to incorporate yield is to calculate current yield and use that as the yield component in your return calculation. To calculate yield, divide the most recent annual dividend by the current price of the stock. ABC Company last paid a dividend of 12 cents per share, so your dividend income is 0.4 percent of the $32 share price—not a significant amount ($0.12 \div 32 = 0.4\%$). When you add the 0.4 percent yield to the initial 15.2 percent appreciation, you arrive at a total return of 15.6 percent. Adding it to the more "accurate" result, the total return for ABC Company comes out to be 16.7 percent, compounded annually. This would be comfortably above our desirable return of 14.9 percent.

Average return. Another return calculation may be of interest to you: the *projected average return*. This is the same as the total return calculation, except that the projected price (FV) in the equation is calculated by multiplying the high earnings by the forecast average PE rather than the forecast high PE. For ABC Company, the projected average return would be 10.3 percent. (See Figure 10.11.) And, using the higher, more-timely earnings value to calculate the average price of 53.71, the total return would be about 11 percent.

No matter how clever I may think I am, I can never seem to sell a stock at its high! It seems as though someone else always gets a higher price for it right after I sell. However, the opportunities I might expect to be able to sell a stock at its average multiple are bound to be more frequent. The projected average return—a total return based upon the lower selling price—is a more conservative view of the future. It's nice to know that I don't have to depend upon selling the stock at a higher-than-average multiple of earnings to make money.

I've set no deal-breaker goal for the average return, but I do feel good if it exceeds the percentage guidelines that I gave you in Chapter 7 (Figure 7.11) for minimum sales growth commensurate with the size of company.

Determining the Potential Risk

Evaluating risk, as does estimating return, also has four logical but simple steps:

1. Estimating the future low PE.
2. Estimating future low earnings.
3. Calculating the potential low price.
4. Calculating the risk index.

Estimating the Future Low PE

You've already estimated the future low PE! When you averaged the lowest half or majority of the low PEs (see Figure 10.7), you were forecasting the low PE. In our example, the forecast low PE is 15.7.

Estimating Future Low Earnings

To estimate the risk, you're going to use the same logic on the downside as you did on the upside to establish a price. Multiply the *lowest* reasonable estimate of future earnings by the *lowest* reasonable multiple of those earnings to come up with a reasonable estimate of the *lowest* price to which you might expect the stock to fall.

First, you need to estimate the lowest earnings you could reasonably expect to be possible in the future. To be on the safe side, *let the earnings for the most recent four quarters* represent the lowest future earnings. How much more conservative can you be? This is a good growth company. You can't expect earnings to be lower in five years than they were during the past 12 months. If they should decline below that figure for very long, you will want out anyway.

Calculating the Potential Low Price

To calculate the risk, you'll have to figure out what the price would be if the company produced the lowest earnings you forecast and the stock sold at the lowest PE you predicted. Simply multiply the low earnings by the low PE, and you'll arrive at your potential low price.

In this example, ABC Company's earnings might remain at $1.37, and its stock could sell at a low multiple of 15.7. The product of the two figures is $21.51—the potential low price. Armed with that downside figure, you can now figure the risk: what you might lose if the stock price should go down to that potential low price instead of going up. The way you'll assess this risk is to calculate the risk index—a comparison of what you have to lose in the worst case versus what you have to gain if all goes well.

Calculating the Risk Index

To calculate the risk index, divide the difference between the current price and the potential low price (your possible loss) by the difference between the potential high price and the potential low price (the "deal"— the range between the best and worst case). The result is the risk index, the percentage of the deal that is risk. We look for a risk index of 25 percent or less, meaning that only a quarter of the proposition or less is risk. We would then have at least 75 percent to gain versus at most 25 percent to lose; so the reward is at least three times the risk.

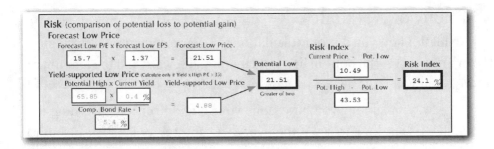

Figure 10.12. The Risk Index

As with the historical value ratio (HVR), the benefits of considering the risk fall at both ends of the buy/don't buy spectrum.

In general, the lower the risk, index the better. If your risk is minimal or nonexistent, there is no question that you're better off, *provided that there are no legitimate reasons for the price to be as low as it is or to go lower*.

If the HVR didn't warn you that a company's price is depressed, the low risk index is a last-chance warning. If the HVR did not tell you that the price, expressed as a multiple of earnings, is lower than people have historically been willing to pay for the stock, the risk/reward relationship can tell you that the price simply appears too good to be true! If you find that your risk is extraordinarily low compared with the reward— zero or negative risk—don't buy it unless you can satisfy yourself that the company is just fine, and it's only ignorant investors who are driving the price down (it happens). However, don't be too quick to dismiss the possibility that people who are selling the stock know something you don't! The most important determination, of course, is that you don't buy the stock if there is too great a risk. In fact, it's safe to say that unless the reward is close to three times the risk, you should add the company to your watch list and wait until the price is more favorable.

Let's put theory into practice with ABC Company. First, find the difference between the current price ($32.00) and the potential low price ($21.51). The result is $10.49. Next, calculate the difference between the potential high price ($65.04) and the potential low price ($21.51). That result is $43.53. Divide the first result by the second to arrive at a risk index of 24.1 percent, which is just below our limit of 25 percent. We can therefore conclude that our return of 15.6 (or 16.7) percent, is obtainable with only reasonable risk.

To Buy or Not to Buy

No matter how you do your calculations—using a computer, a calculator, or an abacus—the bottom line is the potential reward and the amount of risk that you must accept to achieve it.

Always assuming you have done your due diligence concerning the quality issues, look to see if the hypothetical total return is sufficient to warrant adding the stock to your portfolio. If the stock appears to be capable of doubling its value in five years, it's probably a good buy.

If you have been cautious enough in your estimates of earnings growth and future PEs, and if the potential reward is at least three times the risk of loss, you'll have no qualms about buying the stock.

Would ABC Company be a good deal at $32? You bet! Suppose, however, that its risk index were a few tenths of a percent above the desired value of 25 percent? This brings up a final point of importance.

Use your good common sense. Investing is far from a precise science. What you lose in accuracy because you're building one estimate upon another, you gain by being conservative in your estimates. If you're careful to take the more cautious choice at every opportunity, you're rarely going to be disappointed at the outcome.

A small difference—a 1-percent difference in the risk index in this case—would translate into less than 50 cents in the share price) is not enough to warrant waiting for the price to be just right.

If the price is more than just a little too high for the value parameters to satisfy you, however, you'll want to complete your study and wait for the price to come down to a more reasonable figure.

What Is the Right Price?

Assuming that a company meets the quality standards, there are really only two criteria with which to determine if the price is right: the *reward* and the *risk*. From the information you've developed in your study, you can easily work backward and calculate the price at which each of those criteria is satisfied.

Some of the software will calculate a reasonable price for you, but it's easy enough to do with your calculator.

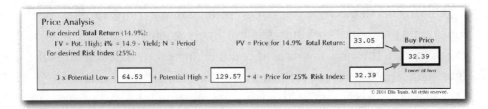

Figure 10.13. Calculating the Buy Price

To satisfy the reward, or total return, requirement, plug the following information into your calculator:

> FV = the potential high price
>
> i% = 14.9 *less the current yield*
>
> N = 5
>
> Solve for PV. This present value is what the price would have to be today to arrive at that result.

For ABC Company:

> FV = 65.04
>
> i% = 14.5
>
> N = 5
>
> Solving for PV, the highest price that could give you the desired return would be $33.05.

Hypothetically, you could double your money every five years if you bought ABC Company at $33.05—$1.05 above its current price.

To satisfy the risk requirement, multiply the potential low price by three, add the potential high price, and divide the result by four. (See Figure 10.13.) The result is $32.39.

The lower of these two prices is the price at which you can feel quite comfortable buying the stock. This is a good price to look for on your watch list.

Remember that prices can fluctuate by as much as 50 percent on either side of their averages during the course of the year; so you might be pleasantly surprised when a price you thought beyond hope just happens to materialize one day.

181

Quality persists. Once you've determined that a company does meet your quality standards, its status is not likely to change—at least for a while. In fact, the only factor that could change your assessment is the data that is reported every three months, so you can be reasonably confident that your assessment will survive at least that long. And there's an 80-percent chance it will last a good deal longer. So it pays you to collect and maintain a "watch list" of good companies and wait for them to hit an attractive price—just have them available should your portfolio management strategy call for selling or replacing one you already own.

Let's Take Stock of What You Know About the Value Issues

The most important task in buying a stock is to determine that the company is a good company in which to own stock for the long term. However, no matter how good the company, if the price of its stock is too high, it's not going to be a good investment.

A stock price must pass two tests to be considered reasonable:

1. The hypothetical total return from the investment must be adequate—enough to contribute to a portfolio average of around 15 percent—sufficient to double its value every five years.

2. The potential gain should be at least three times the potential loss.

To complete these tests, you have learned how to do the following:

> Estimate future sales and earnings growth.

> Estimate future earnings.

> Analyze past PEs (check the HVR).

> Estimate future PEs.

> Forecast the potential high and low prices.

> ► Calculate the potential return.
>
> ► Calculate the potential risk.
>
> ► Calculate a fair price.

If you take each of these steps cautiously and shun excesses, your actual result is likely to be as good or better than the forecast at least four out of five times. And you will have a track record to rival any professional.

As the little cartoon character Porky Pig used to say, "That's all folks!"

That's all there is; there ain't no more!

Well, that's not entirely true. But it's really all you need to build a great portfolio that will meet your expectations handily. However, to maintain that portfolio at peak performance, you will need to manage it well, optimizing its performance and preventing the companies that occasionally go south from damaging it. Portfolio management chores take a minimal amount of time, especially when you consider the value of the results; and, you'll read all about doing them in Chapter 12.

As your experience increases, you'll pick up a lot more useful information on your own. However, I would be remiss if I didn't include in this book some additional tips gleaned from my own experience. You'll find them in Chapter 13. But be sure to heed the warning that accompanies that chapter.

In the next chapter, we'll talk about comparing companies: What happens if you want to pick the best of two or more companies that might be good buys? How do you figure out which company in an industry is the best choice for your investment dollars?

CHAPTER 11

Comparing Companies

S ometimes you will be interested in more than just a single company—or even in a single industry. Occasionally, especially when you first start out, you'll want to consider a number of candidates for selection.

In the process of doing your stock studies, you will have developed information about a number of companies that can then be of value in matching one investment opportunity against others that are competing for your investment dollars.

The job of comparing is so easy that it would be foolish to pass up the chance to make sure the companies you select are the best of your candidates.

Under what circumstances might a comparison be called for?

> **To consider a single stock.** You have studied a stock that you are particularly interested in—perhaps someone mentioned it as a tip or you read about it somewhere—and you are satisfied with its potential. You may want to look at other contenders in the same industry to see if there are any better choices.

> **To select one from a group of stocks.** You have studied a group of companies but have the money to buy only one or two for the moment. You will want to know which of them to select.

> **To study an industry.** You want to look at a particular industry that has attracted your attention to see which companies within it are the most attractive investments. You will, of course, need to perform the quality and value checks on each of the companies to develop the data necessary for meaningful comparison.

> **To select from among club choices.** You are in an investment club and want to settle on the best prospect from among several presented to the group.

> **To decide whether to switch to a different stock.** In the next chapter, you'll learn that there will be times when you should replace one stock with another that is of equal or better quality but that has a better potential for return. You may wish to compare the company you already own with one or more other companies to see if your portfolio could benefit from the swap.

For these or other reasons, you may find it desirable to compare investment opportunities with one another. This chapter will help you with that.

Probably the easiest way to compare companies is with a computerized spreadsheet program such as Microsoft Excel or with one of the software packages that are described in Appendix B. If you have no computer, you can make your comparisons on a piece of lined paper.

Creating a Comparison Worksheet

On a comparison worksheet (created with a computer spreadsheet program or on a piece of paper), you're going to list the criteria you will use for comparison along the left side of the page. You'll provide a column heading at the top of the page for each of the companies you wish to compare. Then you'll enter the information from your completed stock studies in the appropriate spaces and compare the stocks according to your criteria, circling or otherwise marking the winner or winners for each. The company with the most marks will probably—but not necessarily—be your best choice.

This simple procedure is a good starting place for a decision. With thoughtful deliberation about how much weight to give each criterion, and with some thought about the significance of other, subjective issues I'll talk about in the following pages, the worksheet can be of great help in making your decision.

Choosing and Prioritizing Your Comparison Criteria

The criteria that you will use for your comparisons will be pretty much the same as those you used for your stock studies, although you may decide to incorporate additional criteria of your own. You should give first priority to the quality issues, then consider the value issues.

It's entirely possible that you will find a company whose quality criteria are more favorable than those of another—its growth and stability are more impressive—but whose stock is selling for a little higher price than you feel you should pay, whereas the other is a bargain at the moment.

Naturally, you'll want to weigh those considerations carefully, and you could be confronted with a dilemma: Should you buy a company of suitable quality at a great price? Or should you buy a company of better quality at a less attractive price? It could be a tough call. Perhaps the answer will lie in the urgency. Can you afford to wait for the price to come down on the better-quality stock? Some of the additional criteria that will be factored into your comparison are informational, not quantitative. For example, even if you're not comparing companies within a specific industry but are simply looking for the best investment, the industry may still have a place in your decision. If the numbers are similar, you may want to give the edge to a company in a more vital or secure industry, depending upon your personal experience, perceptions, or interests. Quantitative measures aren't the only useful comparative criteria.

Setting Up Your Worksheet

Here's a list of basic criteria that you should list on your comparison worksheet. I have briefly described each item and have indicated whether

187

the "winner" will have the higher or lower value for that criterion compared with its competitors. I have also referred to the chapter in this book where you can review each item.

Quality

Historical sales growth. (Chapter 7)   (Higher)
　　Growth rate of sales *for relevant years*.

Historical earnings growth. (Chapter 7)   (Higher)
　　Growth rate of earnings *for relevant years*.

Future sales growth. (Chapter 10)   (Higher)
　　Your estimate of future sales growth.

Future earnings growth. (Chapter 10)   (Higher)
　　Your estimate of future earnings growth.

Sales predictability. (Chapter 8)   (Higher)
　　Using the computer you will find the value of R^2. In the jargon of statisticians, R^2 is the *coefficient of determination*, which measures on a scale from zero to one the extent to which the plotted points on which a trend line is based fall on, close to, or well away from that line. If all of the points lie on the trend line, R^2 is 1 (or 100 percent). If none are close, R^2 approaches zero. Most financial software products (including the compact disk that comes with this book) will provide you with the R^2 value for trend lines you are evaluating.

　　If you are working manually, you will make a subjective judgment about sales predictability based on your visual assessment of the degree to which the growth line approaches your goal of monotonous excellence. A 10 would indicate a perfectly straight growth line, and a one would be assigned to a line that describes wildly fluctuating growth.

Earnings predictability. (Chapter 7)   (Higher)

Evaluated in the same way as sales predictability.

Note: *Value Line* has a measurement called "Earnings Predictability" that doesn't relate directly to the stability criteria we've discussed; still, *Value Line* users may apply that measurement here because it addresses essentially the same issues.

Average profit margin. (Chapter 9)   (Higher)

The average of the last five years of pretax profit margins.

Profit Margin Stability. (Chapter 10)   (Higher)

Evaluated subjectively in the same way as sales predictability.

Trend in Profit Margins. (Chapter 10)   (The more

A comparison of the most recent year's profit margin positive,
with the average profit margin. If the most recent year is the better)
higher than the average, the trend is up. Record it as
("++," "+," "=," "–," or "––").

Value

Current PE. (Chapter 10)   (Lower)

Calculated using the most recent four quarters of earnings.

Historical value ratio (HVR). (Chapter 10)   (Lower, if

Current PE compared to signature PE.   above 85)

Risk index. (Chapter 10)   (Lower)

Risk of loss from decline in price, expressed as a percentage of the range between the forecast high and low price.

Total Return. (Chapter 10)   (Higher)

Compounded appreciation and income if stock were to sell at the high PE.

Average Return. (Chapter 10)   (Higher)

Compounded appreciation and income if stock were to sell at the average PE.

Miscellaneous Information

Current price. (N/A)

Number of shares you can buy with the fixed amount (N/A)
of money you would like to spend.

Industry. (N/A)

Exchange where stock is traded. (N/A)

As you go along, you may come up with other items that are of importance to you and can have a bearing on your decision. Don't hesitate to list and prioritize additional criteria.

Be sure to put the name and/or ticker symbol of the company at the top of the list so you can easily identify it as you add the data. If you are listing the criteria by hand, you might want to numerically prioritize them and then list them in order of importance. If you create the list on your computer using a spreadsheet program, you can simply type in your criteria, assign each a number indicating its level of priority, then sort the list when you are finished.

When you've completed your prioritized list, make a master copy of it from which you can run copies from time to time so you won't have to construct the list again. If you're using a computer, it's simple enough to save the spreadsheet as a template and bring up a fresh document each time you perform your comparisons.

Selecting Stocks to Compare

Before you select stocks to compare, eliminate any companies that fall below your baseline quality standards. Then determine what your objective is in making your comparison.

Is it important to you that the companies you compare be in the same industry? Or are you simply looking for the best overall investment? You may just want to be sure that the company you've tentatively chosen is the best in its industry. Or it may be that your portfolio's diversification goals suggest that you add a company in a particular economic sector or industry.

One advantage of comparing companies in similar industries is that comparisons on some of the criteria may be valid only within an industry. For example, a company's profit margins will be on an "apples to apples" basis when you are comparing companies within the same industry, but profit margin comparisons will be irrelevant if you are considering companies in different industries. You simply can't compare Microsoft's profit margins with Home Depot's. However, you can compare the *trend* in profit margins to determine whether each company is controlling its costs properly.

There are some very good reasons to compare companies within a single industry, but this isn't essential if your objective is to come up with the most profitable option regardless of industry.

How many stocks should you compare? No more than five. If you work with more than five, the comparison becomes both unwieldy and less meaningful; you'll be conducting a screening exercise rather than a comparison, and you'll have a tough time selecting the winner.

Analyzing the Results

Once you've selected stocks to compare, it's time to enter the result from the completed stock study for each criterion in a column under the appropriate company's name and ticker symbol. When you have finished, you will have a column of significant numbers and other data for each of the companies side by side.

The next step is to compare each of the variables, circling or otherwise marking the favorable values. You should circle more than one company's result for a criterion when the values are not too far apart. It's less important to pick a single winner in each of the categories than it is to pick the values that seem better than most of the others.

The trouble with computer programs that do all of this for you is that they mark only the highest value, no matter how close the winner is to the runner-up. Sometimes a company that is perfectly good will lose the contest by a tiny fraction of a number.

The lesson here is to be judicious about selecting the winners. For the comparison to be most effective and do you the most good, you should ponder each item and make a conscious decision about its meaning and importance. Many investors foolishly look at each item, decide whether higher or lower is better, and circle the highest or lowest value on that line. The wisest approach is to consciously consider each criterion. Remind yourself about what makes it important to you.

And think about the significance of half a percent or a couple of pennies—or a couple of million dollars—when you decide whether or not to circle a value.

If you've marked your values properly, you will have a number of rows in which there are several marks—in fact, some rows may have a mark for every company.

Don't play favorites! It's easy to yield to temptation and favor the company you started with. (Suppose you're a member of an investment club and are comparing your own candidate with the companies that others have proposed. It's not hard to imagine succumbing to the temptation to play favorites, but the rest of the members probably won't let you get away with it!)

Here's a trick: Don't use any rhyme or reason for the order in which you assign the companies to the columns. Or assign them alphabetically. Just don't follow the normal instinct and put the stock you first decided to study in the first column. One fellow I know just calls the companies "A," "B," "C," and so on. You'd be surprised at how much better a job you'll do of comparing the variables if you judge the values on their merits alone rather than associating them with particular companies.

When you've finished marking the data, you may then add up the marks and see which companies come out with the greatest number. If your criteria are relatively few, you'll have a pretty good start for deciding which company with which you will want to go.

It's also a good idea to make room on your comparison worksheet for notes so that you can look back and remember the things you considered when you made your decision.

It's important not to select a company solely because it's numerically superior to the others. The numbers serve only as a guide. The most important judgment is your overall subjective assessment. You might prefer industries you're familiar with and companies whose stores you shop in and are impressed with.

These and other subjective criteria should be used for tiebreakers if you come up with two or more companies that are close on the quantitative measures.

Comparison Worksheet										
		Company 1		Company 2		Company 3		Company 4		Company 5
Company		Home Depot		Lowes Com.		Kohl's Corp.		Dollar Tree		Walgreen
Ticker		HD		LOW		KSS		DLTR		WAG
Quality										
Historical sales growth		10.0%		16.4%		12.7%		18.3%	x	13.3%	
Historical earnings growth		17.5%		25.1%	x	-7.5%		11.9%		14.3%	
Future sales growth		9.7%		16.3%		12.6%		17.8%	x	13.3%	
Future earnings growth		9.7%		16.3%	x	-7.1%		10.8%		13.3%	
Sales predictability		96.9		99.4		99.1		97.4		99.9	x
Earnings predictability		97.0		99.4		95.5		91.1		99.6	x
Average pretax profit margin		9.8		7.9		10.1		11.3	x	5.7	
Profit margin stability		9		9		7		7		10	x
Profit margin trend		+	x	++	x	-		-		=	x
Value										
Current PE		18.3		21.1		26.7		17.5	x	29.4	
Historical value ratio (HVR)		59.0	x	90.0		82.0		70.0		95.0	
Total return		22.3%		23.5%		-7.3%		27.3%	x	10.9%	
Average return		15.9%		17.5%		-11.7%		17.8%	x	5.9%	
Risk index		7.5%	x	14.0%		413.9%		12.3%		47.1%	
Miscellaneous										
Current price		38.7		53.2		49.48		27.42		37.01	
Number of shares $1,000 will buy		25.8		18.8		20.2		36.5		27.0	
Industry		Retail		Retail		Retail		Retail		Retail	
Where traded		NYSE		NYSE		NYSE		NASDAQ		NYSE	
Scores			3		3		0		6		4

DLTR scored the most points, but it's obvious that those points arose from prematurely jumping over the "barbed wire fence." The quality issues have driven the price down.

WAG is the most stable but has grown too large to provide sufficient growth. This leaves the hot competitors, HD and LOW. Both are excellent; but LOW has the edge. Its growth is slightly higher than that of HD; and its total return is projected higher. The clincher is the HVR which suggests that someone knows something about HD that I don't know.

Figure 11.1. A Simple Comparison of Five Retailers

Comparison can be fun as well as valuable. (See Figure 11.1.) There have been times I've started the exercise with a successful stock study and scant interest in going through the motions of checking to see if I might have overlooked something better, only to find that there was an alternative that was clearly superior. Often, you'll find that the "good deal" you contemplated buying has given way to a "great deal"—just because you were objective enough to keep an open mind and take a look.

Let's Take Stock of What You Know About Comparing Companies

> There are times when it's a good idea to compare one investment opportunity with another in order to select the best alternative.

> The easiest way to compare companies is to select and prioritize the essential criteria and place the companies' performance on the criteria side by side for analysis.

> Some criteria are merely informational, not quantitative.

> Minor numerical differences are not important in weighing one company's performance against another.

> Marking the winning numbers and counting those marks is a good starting point for making a decision, but subjective judgment that includes other considerations such as the company's industry or the quality of your own experience with the company should also influence your final judgment.

CHAPTER 12

Managing Your Portfolio

Before I tackle the issue of portfolio management, I need to clarify just what *portfolio management* really means, because there are a few misconceptions.

What Is Portfolio Management—Really?

Many folks think that *portfolio management* means tracking their portfolio—watching the prices and checking how much they've gained or lost on their holdings.

It's not. Tracking merely tells you how well or poorly you may have managed your portfolio—after the fact. Portfolio management is a proactive process; it involves taking some action.

Other investors believe that they're managing their portfolios when they watch the market and then sell stocks when prices reach predefined targets or when returns exceed predefined goals. Wrong again! Let me say emphatically that, contrary to popular opinion, portfolio management does *not* require you to sell the stocks whose prices move into disappointing territory or languish there.

All of your stocks can fit that description from time to time—and probably will—without any long-term consequence to fret about. As I've said elsewhere, excursions of 50 percent on either side of the average price are not at all unusual in the best of times, and for the best of stocks.

If all things were textbook-perfect, the price of each of your stocks would grow in lockstep with earnings, the PE would hover closely around the signature PE, and at any time you would be able to sell the stock at the same multiple of earnings that you paid for it—perhaps more—and make a tidy profit.

But that would be against the law—Murphy's Law: If something can go wrong, it will. Remember that, in the short term, prices are driven by investors' whims and by a whole variety of hot issues that can either warm investors' hearts or ignite the flames of discontent.

Actual fundamentals such as sales, pretax profit, and earnings are reported only quarterly, so changes in the fundamentals aren't responsible for short-term price fluctuations. Rumors, stories, insider tips, analysts' upgrades or downgrades, and other "soft" stuff, as opposed to hard facts, drive short-term price changes. And some of that soft stuff can influence your stocks' prices long enough to challenge your patience.

The soft stuff can be related to a particular company (a rumor about a change in management), a single industry (rumors of new competitive technology that threatens the existing participants), a market sector (a small increase in interest rates that can affect consumer cyclicals), or the market as a whole (consensus by analysts that the sky is falling after the chairman of the Federal Reserve Board makes a speech).

In Chapter 4, when I was discussing the character of the PE, I stated that "any price (PE) movement that is not related to the company's earnings is transient. If the stories—not the numbers—cause the price to move, the change won't last. What goes up will come down, and what goes down will come up."

I hope this statement will fortify you with abundant patience when prices remain depressed for long periods—sometimes very long periods—as they inevitably will. At such times, you might want to repeat it to yourself as a mantra to help bolster your confidence that prices will eventually return to the fair and reasonable state as a rational multiple of earnings. (You should also repeat the mantra daily when prices balloon to way above where they should be for a very long time.)

Rational Value

A very good way to keep your head up when the market sags and to keep your feet on the ground when shares are overvalued is to calculate the *rational value* of your portfolio. Whereas the historical value ratio (HVR) measures how closely the going price of a dollar's worth of earnings matches the price investors have typically paid in the past, the rational value tells you the price of your holdings if the current PE were to match that signature PE. In other words, if investors were perfectly rational and were basing their buy and sell decisions strictly on the company's earnings, how much would they pay for the shares? What would be the rational price?

Calculating the rational price is a simple matter of dividing the current price by the company's HVR. So, if we're in the middle of a bubble, XYZ Company is selling for $75, and the HVR of XYZ Company is 150 percent, the rational price would be $50 (75 ÷ 1.5). Or, in the middle of a market slump, let's say that XYZ is selling for $25 and the HVR were 50 percent, then the rational price would again be $50 (25 ÷ .50). To determine the rational value of XYZ Company in your portfolio, simply multiply the rational price times the number of shares you own.

If you calculate the rational value of your entire portfolio (the sum of the rational values of each of your holdings), you will be able to see what your portfolio is really worth, based on the value of the companies' earnings, and you can then get a good picture of whether the market is overvaluing or undervaluing your holdings. More important, you'll be able to sit tight in down markets and wait for the herd to recognize the true value of your stocks and reward them accordingly. In a bubble, you'll be able to see what stocks are so overvalued they might better be replaced by others that can offer a better return.

In either case, you'll have some valuable insight into what your portfolio is really worth and be less inclined to worry about what the herd, acting irrationally at that moment, is doing and how it affects your portfolio.

You will find, in fact, that a time of price decline offers a good opportunity to add to your position, provided the company continues to operate as you had hoped. Stock prices retreat because of declines in investor confidence, and investor loss of confidence in excellent companies is groundless far more often than it's justified.

197

You might argue that the landscape is littered with the remains of companies in which investors lost confidence for good reason. But such companies don't usually qualify as quality companies. Or if they were quality companies at some point, they would be among that 20 percent of companies that fall by the wayside for reasons that were simply unpredictable.

To be sure, portfolio management is the practice of monitoring your portfolio and taking whatever actions are necessary to enhance its performance. But watching the daily stock prices is not where it's at. Warren Buffett has made the point often that he would be perfectly content if the market closed as soon as he bought a stock and didn't open again until he was ready to sell it! Although it's impossible for that to happen in the real world, there's nothing to prevent you from pretending that it happens just that way.

In a very real sense, when you buy stocks you buy companies—or at least shares in them. So portfolio management involves monitoring the companies, not their stock prices. This is a major distinction and one that you must embrace.

The Size of Your Portfolio

You now know how to intelligently select the stocks that can help you accumulate substantial wealth over the years. Hopefully you're going to put these methods into practice and build a strong portfolio of somewhere between 10 and 25 stocks—although there's no hard-and-fast rule about how many you should own. If you own 10 or 11 stocks, you have enough baskets for your eggs to ward off a calamity. Beyond that, it's all a matter of your comfort level—and your equipment.

The best rule of thumb is to hold no more companies than you can easily keep track of. This number can vary depending upon whether you do all of your chores by hand, as many people have over the past half century, or on a computer, as most do now. Needless to say, it's a whole lot easier to keep track of stocks when the work is automated. Computerized portfolio management is so much easier, faster, and more accurate than the manual alternative.

However you keep track of your holdings, one of the best things about the technamental approach is that your portfolio management tasks will be far less demanding than they would be if you were a trader or even just a longer-term short-term investor.

Deciding When to Sell

When should you sell your stocks? At what point should you take your profit and get out? The answers to these questions are "never" and "never," respectively.

Well, that's not entirely true. There are, in fact, three occasions when you might want or need to sell your stock.

1. If you want the money—or need it—you'll obviously have to sell your stock to get it.

2. You may discover that you have one of the one-out-of-five companies that the Rule of Five warns you about. You'll want to get rid of it before it does serious damage to your portfolio.

3. You should always have an open mind about replacing one of your stocks with another of equal or better quality and a better potential for return. Replacement may be a good strategy if the price of one of your stocks has been bid up so high as to offer little or no return based on further earnings growth.

Scenarios two and three involve, respectively, the *defensive* and *offensive* portfolio management strategies that I'm going to tell you about. Beyond these three situations, for all practical purposes there are few good reasons to sell your stock.

You're investing for the long haul. And the beautiful part of this discipline is that, over the years, most of the stocks you buy will do just fine—even if you put them in a drawer and forget that you own them! You will have selected companies that can and will continue to grow their earnings. If that earnings growth deserves nearly as much investor confidence as it did when you bought into the companies, your stocks' value will grow right along with the growth of those earnings forever—or for a lot of years, anyway.

But if you *don't* just throw your stocks in a drawer and forget about them, you can do a lot better.

Defensive Strategy

To *defend* is to protect from harm. In a ball game, it also means to prevent loss. Each of these meanings is apropos and both denote a degree of urgency.

A defensive strategy is necessary to protect your portfolio from harm and to prevent loss. Your goal is for your portfolio to average at least a 15-percent return, and you can't afford to retain for too long any bad apples that risk your achievement of that result.

Pursuing a defensive strategy is not very time-consuming. However, it's mandatory that you do spend the little time required to do this job— if you're intent on accumulating wealth.

Some people consider a glass half-full, and some consider it half-empty. It's the same way with the Rule of Five. To the pessimist it means, "For every five stocks you own, one will go bad." When I cite the very same statistic, my preference is to say, "For every five stocks you own, four will do just fine—one of them much better than you expect." I suppose I tend to be the optimist.

Defensive portfolio management strategy, however, deals with the stocks about which the pessimists wring their hands. The objective of defensive strategy is to protect your portfolio from being damaged by companies that, for no predictable reason, fail to perform as you had expected—or that fall from grace after having performed well for a while.

Defensive strategy deals strictly with quality; it has nothing to do with value issues, which *are* price related. I'll talk about the value issues when I discuss offensive strategy.

As long as your companies continue to grow their sales and earnings nearly every quarter at about the rate you have forecast, you have nothing to be concerned about. Unlike the trader who sweats out every moment-to-moment fluctuation of the price, you're concerned only with the long term and with continuing growth in the earnings of the company. Remember: When earnings grow and are multiplied by a reasonable PE, you'll see a continuing increase in the stock's value.

What to Look For

So what do you look for when you pursue a defensive strategy? Look at each company's sales, earnings, and pretax profit each quarter, comparing them with the figures from the same period the previous year. Calculate the percentage change for each item and check to be sure that it is close to the growth rate you expected when you bought the stock.

Check each company's sales first. This should be the most stable figure, so, if sales growth has slipped below your expectations, you know something of major significance is the cause.

Next, examine pretax profit to see if it's growing at the rate that you expected earnings to grow. This is the most important item after sales: Declines in profit growth will ultimately affect earnings, but companies can sometimes stave off the impact on earnings for a quarter or two by making adjustments in their provision for income taxes and in the number of shares outstanding. If you're lucky, when you check pretax profit you can spot a problem before it reaches the bottom line.

If you do catch a problem with pretax profit before it reaches the earnings line, you may be able to respond before most other investors see and react to the coming, unfavorable earnings report; you may be able to get out without the loss you might have taken if you were to wait until the earnings took the hit and the rest of the pack responded.

After checking for a decline in sales and pretax profit, do the same for earnings growth. By the time the problem shows up in the earnings, it may be too late to save much money. On the other hand, if the problem is not a long-term, serious one, it may provide you with a great opportunity to buy some more.

What to Do if You Detect a Decline

What should you do if you find a disappointment in any of these statistics? Should you put in a sell order right away? Not at all! You didn't subject the company to all those tests for nothing! And you don't want to sell it without a very good reason. After all, the company's management has proven itself able to solve problems in the past. This may be only a single event. One bad quarter does not a loser make.

I prefer to look at the trailing 12 months for sales, pretax profit, and earnings, comparing the sum of the most recent four quarters with the comparable period from the previous year. This dampens out the effects of a single quarter and, unless a series of poor quarters has dragged the four quarters down appreciably—or unless there's a drastic decline in one or more of those quarters—the alarm is not likely to go off with such sensitivity and I'm not as likely to be sidetracked by momentary "hiccups."

Remember that companies whose growth has been extraordinary and that are still early in their life cycles will experience slowing growth rates. This shouldn't be alarming. Compare the growth with your expectations, not with the company's historical rate of growth. This is precisely why you selected a *sustainable* growth rate for your expected future growth when you decided to buy the stock.

If a company has been growing its sales, pretax profit, or earnings at more than 20 percent, even for an extended period of time, you shouldn't worry if its growth slows to a more reasonable rate. It's only when the growth rate continues to fall below your expectations that you need have any concern. On the other hand, as with any other falling object, if growth is falling fast, you should take its momentum into account when you decide on a course of action. You might benefit from reevaluating the stock and making a more modest growth rate prediction. Certainly it would behoove you to look closely at the reasons for the declines in sales, pretax profit, or earnings.

If the decline in growth is not huge but is still enough to claim your attention, give the stock another quarter to recover. You shouldn't be alarmed unless or until at least two consecutive quarters are disappointing.

Anything can happen at any time, and management may need a quarter or two to deal with an unexpected turn of events. It's too much to expect a company to enjoy total serenity and perpetual good times. Important to you is the way management handles adversities when they do arise. You've taken pains to "hire" a management that's competent to take problems in their stride when they arise, not just to go with the flow when everything's hunky-dory. Unless the problem is serious and long-term in nature—likely to be beyond management's ability to fix it—it's appropriate to let management have a shot at making the repairs before you do anything rash.

A decline in growth to a level below your expectations is certainly a red flag, however. If the problem repeats itself two quarters in a row, or if the decline is substantial—for example, the company *lost* 5 percent instead of growing at 15 percent—it's time to do something about it.

What action should you take? Should you sell the stock? Not necessarily. The first thing you should do is to do your research. Find out what the company says about the reasons for the decline. In its quarterly report the company has likely offered some explanation for the change.

Go up on the Internet, either to the company's own Website or to the host of sites that offer current news. You'll find the news release announcing the quarterly results among those news items. Read it and consider how plausible the explanation sounds. Submit it to the test of your own common sense.

If you don't understand the company's explanation—if it sounds like so much gobbledygook to you—don't be afraid to challenge it. Call the company's investor-relations person (you should be able to find the number on the company's Website) and request a clear explanation. It doesn't matter how few shares you hold. You are one of the owners, and you have a right to an explanation—in a fashion that's understandable to you.

I've found that most investor-relations people are patient and eager to please shareholders. The enlightened ones recognize that, although individual and club investors may not buy as many shares as institutional investors do, they are collectively the most valuable stockholders. Individual and club investors are neither as fickle nor as disloyal as the institutional investors who play the pro game on Wall Street.

A company that has a strong base of individual investors in it for the long term benefits in a great many ways. The best investor-relations professionals treasure such stockholders because the stability they bring makes the company's shares more sought-after and its new issues easier to sell.

Sources of Information

Where should you obtain the periodic information you need for your defensive strategy? In the first edition of this book I suggested that you request the companies to send you their quarterly reports. However, with the advent of the Internet, most companies have cut back on the cost of printing and mailing those reports and you can find them with just a few mouse-clicks. There is no need to look at any hard-copy data when you can so easily bring it up on the Web.

Far and away the best site, as far as I'm concerned, is Reuters (*www.reuters.com*). There you will find, free of charge, a "one-stop shopping" source of information that should satisfy most of your research needs as well as provide the raw data for your scrutiny. Another excellent source of information is Yahoo Finance (*finance.yahoo.com*). Both of these sources—and there are many more—provide not only the raw data but the latest news releases, analysts' comments, and a variety of other data and opinion that is useful in doing your research.

Draw up a schedule so that you'll know when to look for the quarterly reports. Such a schedule will set you free because the rest of the time you'll know that you have no pressing portfolio management chores. Defensive strategy is crucial to protect your portfolio from harm, but it's not onerous to implement because you need only worry about each company four times a year.

Approximately 60 percent of publicly traded companies match their fiscal years with the calendar year. This means that their books are closed at the end of March, June, September, and December, with the fiscal year ending on December 31st. Many retailers close their books at the end of January rather than the end of December so they can focus all of their resources on the intense activity that accompanies the holiday season and can include that activity in the year-end results.

More than half of the remaining companies close their fiscal years in the middle of the year, with the rest scattered fairly evenly throughout the rest of the year for one reason or another.

A company can't complete its financial statements without completing a number of accounting chores after the period ends, so there is a certain amount of lead time required before their results are reported. You can't expect on April 1st to read a company's earnings report for the quarter ending March 31st—even on the Internet.

The Securities and Exchange Commission (SEC) requires all publicly traded companies with more than 500 shareholders and $10 million in assets (you're not likely to be interested in any smaller companies) to report their quarterly results (called 10-Qs) within 45 days following the end of each quarter and their audited annual results (called 10-Ks) within 90 days following the end of the fiscal year. (And most companies take all of the time allowed.)

The most reliable source for the final figures for each period is the SEC, which reports the figures on its EDGAR Website (*www.sec.gov/*). Of course, most companies provide their financial information on their own Websites. As I mentioned, I'm partial to Reuters (*www.reuters.com*) because it provides much, much more information than just the earnings reports. If you are interested in researching sites you can access for company-specific information of all kinds, you can go to DailyStocks (*www.dailystocks.com*) and explore the wide variety of Website links available there.

The final defensive consideration is to recognize that the money you take out of a poor stock is not going to do you any good if it's not reinvested in a better one. So if you're going to take your money out, go back to your stock studies to find another place to put it. This is where the creation and maintenance of a watch list will be of real benefit to you. The moment you need to find another stock, you'll have one handy. That's important! Money not invested is likely to be *losing* ground. You can't win if you don't play!

Offensive Strategy

Now that you know how to keep from losing the game on defense, let's take a few minutes to talk about winning it on offense.

Offensive strategy doesn't share the urgency of defense. Here, you're concerned not so much with preventing loss or protecting your portfolio from harm as you are with enhancing the value of your holdings. You can implement your offensive strategy whenever the spirit moves you.

Offensive strategy involves analyzing the companies whose stock you hold to determine whether their potential return remains satisfactory and if the risk required to obtain it is still reasonable. Obviously you bought your stocks with the idea in mind that their prices would go up over time. And, sure enough, they did! Isn't that the idea? For your stocks to grow and continue growing in value? Of course it is!

In discussing defensive strategies, I made the point that nothing ever goes textbook perfect and that prices can fall, and even stay down for a long time, for a variety of reasons other than the fundamentals. The same applies on the upside. Stock prices can go up for reasons other than the fundamentals. Investor confidence can be buoyed up by a variety of events that affect the company, the industry, the market sector, or the market as a whole—or speculation about how those events will affect the price of the stock.

More often than is the case on the downside, the "hot" issues that warm investors' hearts are not related to the fundamentals at all. It's rare, of course, to see spectacularly pleasant surprises rather than unpleasant ones surfacing in the earnings reports. But it's not at all unusual to see prices temporarily driven sky-high by stories and rumors about the company, its industry, or the economy.

And then there are times when the market as a whole is inflated well beyond the bounds of common sense. Stimulated by a mix of economic euphoria, a surplus of money in the hands of those who don't know what to do with it, and a belief that the law against free lunches has been repealed, along will come extraordinary times such as the dot-com bubble of the 1990s.

Under any such circumstances, it's entirely possible for the price of one or more of your stocks to rise too much. If the price is so high that you would be hard put to justify adding the stock to your portfolio if you didn't already own it, you might now find it difficult to justify keeping it.

All of the price-dependent value measurements you made when you first considered buying a stock are still valid for judging the stock's current potential to increase in value. The higher the price, the less the potential gain. This means that a stock whose price has performed better than you had hoped may suffer because its *potential* is not as good as it would be if the price were lower.

Confused? Let's back up a bit, then. First of all, once you buy a stock, the next likely question is when you should sell it. Portfolio management certainly deals with that question.

Defensive strategy, you learned, is both urgent and necessary. You *must* sell your potential losers—companies whose quality standards have slipped—or they can wreak havoc with your portfolio. Defensive strategy is easy enough to understand and implement. It takes little time and the process is pretty cut-and-dried.

But making money is quite different from not losing it. And you're now concerned with when to sell your stocks to make the most money.

The Role of the Price

As a long-term investor, you should set no price goals. Yes, you've anticipated what the price of a stock might be in five years, but *that number is a moving target*! You should push your time horizon out five years from whatever point in time you look at your investments or prospective investments. No matter when you look at a stock or at your portfolio as a whole, you should be concerned with five years *from that moment.* (You should actually be concerned with 10, 20, or more years out, but your five-year benchmark is sufficient to move your estimates beyond the point where the price should be affected by short-term volatility.)

Let's say that you own a wonderful company and its fundamentals are performing as well as or better than you hoped they would. Now the price has gone up to where you're tempted to take your profit and hit the road. Whoa! Stop! Time out!

What are you going to do with the money? Spend it? Or are you going to try to find another investment that will do as well for you as that one did? Chances are, you're going to look for another winner—or you should, unless you need or want the money for some immediate purpose.

But hold on a minute! What's wrong with the company that you're thinking about selling? Is it not still a good company? Is it not still churning out those earnings the same way you would want its replacement to? Is the company not still top-notch? Does it not meet all of the criteria that you would hope a new investment would—except for the current price? If it does, why sell it?

If you sell the stock, you're going to have to pay taxes on the gain plus the commissions on both that sale and the new purchase. These expenses erode the amount of money you can invest in the new stock. Put those things all together, and you'll have to find some other compelling reason for selling, because capturing the profit isn't a good enough reason. That company still has a great potential for you!

207

Think about it: When you sell your winners, what do you have left? You're left with a portfolio full of losers! And that's not too smart, is it? So read my lips. Never, never, never, never sell a stock because of the price! Is that clear enough?

Replacing, Not Selling

"Okay," you might say, "if I'm supposed to sell only if I need or want the money or if the company goes bad, perhaps I'll never need to think about selling at all." As I've said, low or high, the price should never be a consideration for selling. However, there's a whale of a distinction between *selling* and *replacing*—an important difference I hope to make clear now.

The price is decidedly not a criterion for selling. But, return and risk—both functions of the current price—are very valid criteria for *replacing* a stock.

You did your homework to find the stock. It's performed as well as or better than you expected. You've made money on it so far—at least on paper. You will have to pay taxes and commissions if you sell it. So when do you put your offensive strategy to work?

Your offensive portfolio management strategy is implemented only when a stock is *overvalued*. How do you know when a stock has become overvalued? A stock *commences* to become overvalued when (1) the potential, hypothetical return over the next five years becomes less than you want it to be; and/or, (2) the risk grows to be greater than the reward.

These criteria are familiar, aren't they? Return is the first consideration. If you're looking for a 15-percent return from a company and the potential return falls below 15 percent, the stock has then *commenced* to become overvalued. Its price has been rising, but the earnings on which the future price will be based have probably stood still; therefore, the potential future price based upon those earnings has not increased—yet.

You encountered the risk-to-reward comparison when you looked at the value issues at the time you purchased the stock. A risk index of 25 percent tells you that the reward is three times the risk. It stands to reason, then, that at a risk index of 50 percent, risk and reward are equal. A risk index above 50 percent indicates that the risk exceeds the reward.

Overvaluation, then, is a matter of degree. A stock can be slightly overvalued or greatly overvalued. Your eagerness to replace the stock should grow, the more overvalued it becomes. But how can you say that at a certain price the stock will become *too* overvalued? That can change tomorrow if new earnings are announced. At the current price, does the stock become sufficiently overvalued to warrant its replacement, especially when taxes and commissions are involved? It's pretty difficult to put in a sell order based on anything so slippery.

One important guideline of offensive portfolio management is simply this: Unless you have found an investment of equal or better quality than the one you now own—one with a greater potential for return and with less risk—you should stick with what you have. Because it's a good-quality company that continues to grow its earnings satisfactorily, you probably won't lose anything. You just won't make any if it's overvalued.

Implementing the Strategy

How, then, do you implement your offensive strategy? In the earlier edition of the book, I advocated taking the time to go through your entire portfolio, redoing your stock studies optimistically, and then replacing those that still provided inadequate return at too high a risk. At that time, the market had pumped up the prices of most stocks and it would have been efficient to go through all of your stocks in this fashion.

In normal times, there's no need to do this for your entire portfolio at once. You can apply this strategy to just those companies that seem to qualify.

As I've said, there is nothing to be gained by looking at your portfolio's prices on a daily basis, except to satisfy your curiosity and to occasionally take satisfaction in your success. You're certainly not going to sell a stock on the basis of a stock's price—low or high.

However, when you're ready to check your portfolio for offensive opportunities, it is then that you should review the prices and note those companies whose prices seem higher than you expected them to be.

For any stock that you think might be selling at an unusually high price, update your stock study, making sure the data is the most recent available and the price is current. Check the total return and the risk. If the risk index is greater than 50 percent and/or the return is significantly below what you expected to achieve with that stock, you will want to revise your stock study to reflect what is actually happening rather than the conservative, understated scenario on which you may have based your purchase decision.

Throughout your stock studies I've cautioned you to be conservative. Our byword has been, "When you come to a fork in the road, turn right!" I've told you that every time you have an estimate to make or a judgment to apply, you should err on the side of underestimating rather than over-estimating. It's certainly better to be safe than sorry, and you will always be happy when things turn out better than you expected them to.

The purpose of underestimating future performance is to avoid the temptation to buy stocks that are less than the best, or to pay more than you should for the ones you do buy. You shouldn't have to rely on perfect performance to realize your objectives.

Once you own the stock, however, the conservative approach is the opposite. It entails being *optimistic* rather than *pessimistic*. Why? Because you should not be in too much of a hurry to sell. The more optimistic you are, within reason, the less likely you are to sell before you should and the more you stand to benefit from superior, actual performance.

There are two opportunities to act on such optimism when redoing your stock studies: reestimating the growth of earnings and reestimating the forecast high and low PEs.

Earnings growth. First look to see whether earnings are growing faster than you had forecast and whether they are growing consistently. Your goal is to compare your estimated rate with the actual rate of growth and to forecast the future growth at a rate somewhere between the two. If the growth appears stable and therefore predictable, split the difference. This will give you something of a cushion should growth commence to slow down.

Thus, if you had estimated earnings to grow at 15 percent and they were actually growing at 30 percent, reestimate earnings growth at around 22 percent. In this exercise, you need not be concerned with the 20 percent cap, although I would not go above 25 or 30 percent at the most, depending on how stable growth might be.

You don't actually expect earnings to continue to grow that fast for the next couple of decades; but you are making allowances for the best possible world rather than the worst in the foreseeable future; and before you incur the cost of commissions and taxes, you'd like to get the most out of the stock you already own.

Forecast PEs. The other opportunity to act optimistically is to reestimate the future PEs. Assuming you have eliminated any irrelevant outliers, average *all* of the remaining high and low PEs, and substitute those averages for the figures you used when you bought the stock.

With these optimistic components, recalculate the high price, low price, and the resulting total return and risk index (of course, if you've done this on the computer, it will be instantaneous). You may then decide whether the new values for return and risk are sufficient to warrant replacing the stock with one that has a better potential return with less risk.

Chances are, you will find that the stock you own will be worth keeping, at least for a while longer. If, however, the return is substantially less than 15 percent and/or risk is still around or above 50 percent, you will want to replace that stock with one of equal or better quality having a better potential return.

So that you will be ready when you need replacements, your best bet is to maintain a watch list of high-quality stocks, any of which you would own if the price were right. If you need a new stock, you can simply put in your order for one on your watch list that is in an appropriate price range.

If you can't find an appropriate replacement, hang on to what you have and keep looking. You could do much worse. Keep an eye on the risk and return. If the return reaches the point where it's less than what you could get from the money market with virtually no risk, then sell your stock and leave the money in your money market account until a persistent search turns up another stock that fits your need.

When you leave the money in the money market account, you have "replaced" the stock with an investment of high quality (with virtually no risk) and a better potential for return. You have not "sold" it. In no case, though, do you want to stay in that situation longer than you have to. The sooner you put your money back to work, the better.

Deciding on a Good Replacement

Remember that it's important that your replacement be of at least as good quality as the company you're replacing or better. It may help you to make a checklist of these quality items and compare them using your current stock studies for the stock you own (with the updated growth rates and PEs) and the one with which you propose to replace it. It may be helpful to list the values for each of these items side by side on that checklist:

> - Strength of historical sales growth.
> - Stability of historical sales growth.
> - Strength of historical earnings growth.
> - Stability of historical earnings growth.
> - Strength of recent (trailing four quarters) sales growth.
> - Strength of recent (trailing four quarters) earnings growth.
> - Trend of profit margins.
> - Strength of profit margins (if the replacement stock is in the same industry).

Only if the replacement stock shows a preponderance of these quality items to be as good or better should you then consider the total return and risk index to see if it would pay you to make the swap.

The Effects of Taxes and Commissions

You may encounter a "headwind" when you sell one stock to buy another. By this I mean that the increase in return to be gained with the new investment must be sufficient to at least overcome the cost of the commissions on the trades and the effect of any taxes that might be incurred, and do so within a reasonable period of time.

However, the impact of these factors is often overstated. Over the long term, commissions, when you can trade nowadays for as little as $4 per trade, have far less impact on the benefit than they used to. Only if you are trading few enough shares for the commission to be a large percentage of the total value of the sale will it be significant. Most of the concerns about the cost of selling and buying are carryovers from the days when commissions for odd lots (fewer than 100 shares) were nearly prohibitive and the commissions on the round lots (100 shares) were size-able. If you are selling at least 100 shares, the effect of commissions on the transaction over the long haul should be negligible, especially if you are using the services of a discount or online broker.

Tax Implications of Replacing Stocks

The tax implications of replacing stocks may not be as straightforward.

If, for example, you have all of your stocks in a tax-deferred portfolio—a conventional IRA, a 401(k), a Roth IRA, or the like—there are really no tax consequences to consider so far as a swap is concerned. You won't pay taxes on your gains until you later withdraw the money. So, with the exception of the minor cost of commissions, there is virtually no penalty for swapping one stock for another within a tax-deferred portfolio.

If you're not in a tax-deferred situation and wish to swap your over-valued stock for another, there is no way to avoid paying a tax on your gain. Hopefully, you will have owned the stock you want to trade long enough for the gain on the sale to be considered as capital gains. The tax you will pay on such gains is lower than your standard income tax. In some cases the capital gains tax amounts to only about half as much as your regular income tax—or even less. At this writing, the capital gains tax is only 15 percent.

The only way you can avoid paying taxes on an investment gain is either to die or to lose the gain. Neither of these alternatives is palatable. So you might as well face it: You're going to pay taxes on the gain at some point, no matter what.

In a tax-deferred portfolio, you can sell the stock and then reinvest all the money you took in from the sale. The entire amount of those pro-ceeds will grow, but you'll pay higher taxes later at the regular rates rather than capital gains rates.

If you have a non-tax-deferred portfolio, you will have to pay the taxes in the near term. This means that, although the cash flow situation in your account may allow you to reinvest the full proceeds from the sale right away, soon you're going to have to use some of those proceeds—or money from somewhere else—to cover those taxes. And whatever the amount of those taxes, the money used to pay them won't be earning money for you.

The bottom line here is that, when you have to sell a stock because its fundamentals are no longer performing as you expected when you bought it, you should do so without hesitation. You need to get rid of the stock before it damages your portfolio's performance—and you need to find a stock to replace it as soon as possible so your money can continue to work for you.

If you wish to replace a stock because the return is insufficient and/or the risk too great, you should wait until you can swap it for a stock of equal or better quality whose potential return is at least 2 to 3 percent greater than that of the stock it replaces. Most often, your selection will produce a substantially greater return because, by the time you have decided to replace the stock, it will likely be well below the 15-percent return that qualifies your new stock for purchase. But even a difference of 2 or 3 percent should be enough to cover the burden of both commissions and taxes on the two transactions over the long term.

Let's Take Stock of What You Know About Portfolio Management Strategies

Two strategies will help you make the most of your investments: a defensive strategy and an offensive strategy.

> ▶ *Defensive strategy* implies preventing damage and deals with the quality issues that you have learned. You detect and replace companies whose growth in the fundamentals—sales, pretax profit, and earnings—fall significantly below the expectations you had when you bought the stock. This way you can avoid serious damage to your portfolio's performance.
>
> Never sell a stock because its price is low and has stayed that way unless the fundamentals justify doing so. If the quality issues remain good, you may wish to take advantage of the opportunity to buy more of it at a bargain price.

➤ *Offensive strategy* deals with the value issues and is less urgent. This strategy involves finding the stocks whose prices have appreciated so much that their potential return and risk are no longer desirable. You'll replace the overvalued stocks with others of equal or higher quality that have a better potential for return. If you fail to find acceptable replacements, you will keep the overvalued stocks until suitable replacements can be found.

You should *never* sell your stock in a good company just because it reaches some arbitrary target price or just to capture profits. Remember: Selling your winners will leave you with only losers.

CHAPTER 13

Finer Points and "Fudge Factors"

So far I've given you strategies that are effective, are easy to implement, and will keep you out of trouble. Now I'm about to share with you some things that may be confusing, sometimes counterproductive, and will possibly get you *into* trouble! As you gain technamental investment experience, you'll find that there are times when one or another of the strict guidelines or rules of thumb that I've given you can be relaxed in favor of a wise alternative. And that's truly the best way for you to discover those things: to grow into them.

These "Finer Points and 'Fudge Factors'" will not do a thing to improve your portfolio's *performance. Some of them will only make it easier for you to justify buying companies that you might otherwise not consider.* And there's a risk that, by using these additional points as a rationale for making such decisions, you might make some bad ones.

Don't be too hasty to add any of these less-conservative practices to your repertoire.

Above all, don't think that you need to know about them or that your investment prowess will suffer if you don't digest and embrace them. These finer points are the stuff of my experience. I would feel that I had short-changed you if I didn't at least put them out there for you to reject or accept as your common sense, experience, or confidence guides you to.

Gathering Data for Nonstandard Industries

Some industries are special and report their revenues or sales differently than do other businesses. A prime example of this is the banking and financial services industry. Especially in this day and age, banks are more than just institutions that borrow your money and lend it. The main product of a bank is money. Because a bank borrows the money it lends, usually from the Federal Reserve, it must pay interest on that money. So, for a bank the conventional way to report revenues is to deduct the interest paid for the money from the interest received from the borrower for that money and report that income as *net interest income*.

Banks are also involved in other profitable enterprises, such as mortgage and credit card servicing and investment brokerage. So banks have other profit centers that contribute to their bottom lines and revenues that must be counted as *non-interest income*.

Another departure from the typical business is the way that banks provide for bad debt. Because banks are highly regulated, they must take special precautions to fulfill their fiduciary responsibility to those whose money with which they work. A portion of revenue is set aside as a *loan loss provision* and must be deducted from revenues reported because it is not available to the bank for any other purpose than to cover bad debt.

Because of all these differences, the most informative way to report bank revenues is to combine net interest income and non-interest income and subtract the loan loss provision from the result.

Most of the data sources provide these items, but not all do. The closer you come to including these three items, the more accurate your revenue analysis will be.

There is another item that is not always available but should be included so that your analysis will be accurate. That is the *tax equivalent adjustment*, an accounting adjustment that factors in the portion of a bank's income that comes from tax-exempt securities and then reports that income as its taxable equivalent. The tax equivalent adjustment is smaller and less important to your analysis than the other elements of revenue, but it is still good to know its value, which should be added to the calculation of revenues if it's readily available.

Sometimes you will find that usable information is reported annually but not on a quarterly basis. The *Value Line Survey* reports only "Loans" instead of the "Net Interest Income" on a quarterly basis. In this case, because quarterly revenues are not used for any calculations, you can use the loan information as just a measure of activity.

Assessing Quality

The two issues that determine the quality of a company, you will remember, are the quality of a company's growth and the ability of a company's management to operate the company efficiently to sustain that growth. Let me add a few comments to what you already know about those items.

Evaluating Growth

Forgiving spikes. Some perfectly good companies have slipped now and then, have had a spike in their corporate lives, or have otherwise faltered and then learned from their mistakes. These companies can be perfectly good investments. Compromising on the straightness of the charted lines just a little can open wide new vistas to you, exploding the number of companies you might consider as candidates.

If you find that a company has had a single event that caused a spike in an otherwise acceptable growth picture, you can probably get away with eliminating it as an outlier and pretending it didn't happen. You might even forgive two or even three such events, but only if they happened quite early in the company's history.

They say that time heals many wounds, and a company that's been able to get back on track and demonstrate that it's there to stay can be treated with respect. On the other hand, if a company's strength or stability has been marginal during the period since those events occurred, you will probably want to avoid investing in it.

As a rule of thumb, if by eliminating the offending data, you increase the slope of the trend line and the rate of growth it describes, you shouldn't do it. If by eliminating that data, the slope declines and the growth rate decreases, you can feel comfortable in doing so.

In a nutshell, a long-ago hiccup that is followed by an exceptionally good run of stable and predictable growth can usually be safely overlooked.

Preview of coming detractions. Comparing the slope of the sales and earnings lines can tell you some interesting things about the direction a company is headed.

Look carefully at the direction of the sales and earnings lines. Are they behaving in concert? Or are they diverging or converging? If the sales and earnings lines run pretty much parallel, you'll know that management is probably controlling its costs efficiently and capably. Barring the repurchase or issuance of shares or the unlikely benefits of a tax break, the profit margins remain fairly stable. Expenses, and therefore profits, are increasing right along with revenues.

But what if earnings are growing either more quickly or more slowly than sales? What can you learn from this? First of all, I believe that plotting pretax profit and the number of shares on your growth chart is well worth the extra time and trouble. Then the questions that are raised when the growth of earnings and sales is dissimilar can be answered at a glance. You will want to notice whether the pretax profit line parallels the sales line or the earnings line. (See Figures 13.1 through 13.4 on page 221.)

If sales are growing at a faster rate than earnings and pretax profit is growing at a rate closer to earnings than to sales (as in Figure 13.1), the profit margin is likely decreasing—a bad sign (or there's been an increase in the tax rate).

If sales are growing at a faster rate than earnings and pretax profit is growing at a rate closer to sales than to earnings (as in Figure 13.2), then the number of shares has been increasing (or there's been an increase in the tax rate).

If earnings are growing at a faster rate than sales and pretax profit is growing at a rate closer to sales than earnings (as in Figure 13.3), then the number of shares has likely been decreasing as the company repurchases them (or there's been a decrease in the tax rate).

If earnings are growing at a faster rate than sales and pretax profit is growing at a rate closer to earnings than to sales (as in Figure 13.4), the profit margin is likely increasing—usually a good sign (or there's been a decrease in the tax rate—still a good sign but not likely, at least for the long term).

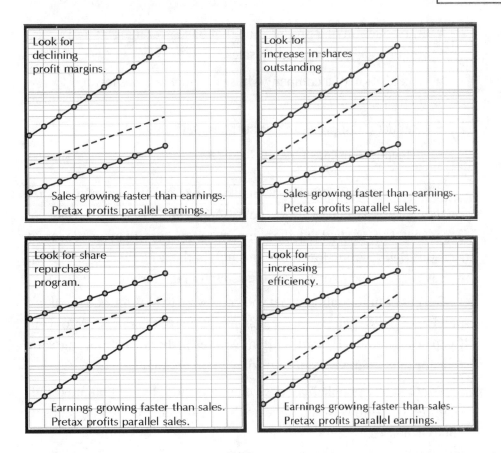

Figures 13.1 through 13.4. Dissimilar Growth Rates for Sales, PTP, and EPS

Changes in the tax rate are the least likely reasons for these dissimilarities in growth rate—especially when the dissimilarities persist for more than a single year. Uncle Sam and his counterparts in the statehouses are not prone to bestowing gifts on industry. But factors such as carryover losses, in which the full tax benefit of a loss could not be claimed in the year of the loss, can distort the otherwise normal role of taxes in the progression from the top to the bottom line.

Evaluating Efficiency

Profit margins. As you become more experienced, you may want to look a little more deeply into companies whose profit margins have declined—especially if you already own them.

There are some scenarios that can produce a reduced margin but be good for the company in the long run and actually represent sound management practices. Such scenarios include:

221

➤ Introduction of a product line that has lower margins and requires higher volumes of sales.

➤ Acquisition of a company whose product line has lower margins.

➤ Reduction of prices to fight off competition.

➤ "Buying" market share.

When you study the facts, you may find to your satisfaction that what you thought was a trend really was not a trend at all and can be overlooked. Or you might be satisfied that the company's management has made sound decisions that result in lower margins but, in the long run, enough of an increase in revenue to overcome the reduction in margin.

But until you're confident that you know what to look for, you shouldn't spend much time trying to make such exceptions to the rule work for you. If you see a reduced profit margin, you're far better off putting your study for that company aside and going on to another company.

Trend. Some people believe that an uptrend is better than no trend. An uptrend certainly would indicate that management is taking steps to reduce expenses.

However, you might ask yourself if the uptrend might not also be an indication that the company's efficiency left something to be desired—that it needed the improvement that is now under way.

Or if the company has already been operating efficiently—its margins are better than average—might not an uptrend result from cost-cutting measures that could prove to be counterproductive? Understanding the causes of an uptrend, as is the case with most of the things your curiosity will lead you to, is a matter of common sense and does not require an MBA. Reading the company's news reports, press releases, and annual reports is a good way to find out about such things as what steps are being taken to cut costs when margins are increasing—or decreasing.

A company that is a leader among its peers in an industry and that has stable profit margins with little or no up trend is probably operating at peak efficiency. There is no reason to worry about it.

Return on equity (ROE). The second item on management's report card is return on equity (ROE)—that is, the return management is able to produce with the equity of the company—the investors' ownership. This is a widely used measure, but I believe that its value to analysts and investors is overrated as it's usually calculated.

Remember that the company's assets—everything it owns (its cash, machines, buildings, computers and other office equipment, airplanes, and so on)—have as their purpose the production of income or the curbing of costs. You would like to assess how effectively the management of your company puts those assets to use.

You must also take into account the obligations that the company has against those assets and reduce the value of the company accordingly.

Return on equity (ROE) is calculated by dividing the company's net profit by its equity. Comparing the profit with the unencumbered assets offers another view of management's effectiveness.

Often ROE is calculated using the company's EPS and its book value. In most cases, either method is fine unless changes have occurred in the number of shares outstanding during the year.

What does ROE tell us? At its simplest, the ROE is supposed to answer this question: Given the amount of money this company is worth after paying off its debt, how much profit does management bring in for every dollar of that value? It's an important measure of management's effectiveness and efficiency. And it's an interesting number because it doesn't matter whether management is using a lot of OPM (other people's money)—or none at all—to bring in the return. ROE just addresses how efficiently management is making use of your share of the company. Debt, or leverage, is simply another tool that management has at its disposal to increase growth and shareholder value.

There is a caveat, however. I believe that return on equity is of practically no value to you unless it's calculated using the equity from the beginning of the period in which the earnings are produced rather than from the end. Unfortunately, however, most of the time you'll find that ROE has been calculated using the equity at the end of the period instead of the beginning—or an average of both. Let me explain.

Return on something usually means the profit you make on whatever that "something" is. If you have $10 and make $1 with it, you figure your return on that $10. Logically, you divide the dollar by the 10-spot and arrive at a 10-percent return. Simple enough.

Return on equity is typically calculated, though, using the book value at the end of the period for which the earnings were reported instead of the book value the company started the period with. All of the earnings not distributed in dividends are therefore retained as a part of that equity or book value. This means that those earnings are a part of both the top and bottom of the ROE equation.

Excluding any consideration of dividend disbursements, calculating ROE this way is the equivalent of dividing that dollar you made by 11 bucks instead of 10—the 11 including the dollar you just made! It's recursive, and therefore, in my opinion, it isn't nearly as meaningful as it should be. Trends tend to be mathematically distorted and of little value.

The problem is compounded if dividends are involved. Company A and Company B both report $1 in earnings for the year, and both start with a book value of $5. Company A retains the entire dollar to equity. Company B, however, pays 20 percent out in dividends, retaining only the remaining 80 cents. Did one company perform better than the other? Calculated using ending equity, the ROE for Company A would be $1 \div 6$, or 16.7 percent. Company B's ROE would be 17.2 percent, which would seem to indicate that the management of the company paying dividends was able to get a better return on its resources than its competitor! Had we calculated the return on beginning equity, both companies would have earned the dollar on $5 for an ROE of 20 percent.

I would likely find the company that did not pay dividends to be more interesting and at least as desirable as the one that did. Certainly the notion that a higher ROE is better (as typically calculated) is not valid in this case.

Many accounting and business schools teach their students to use the *average* of the equity from the beginning and the end. This might be a little better, but in my opinion it still doesn't serve a very useful purpose for you. The potential distortion is merely cut in half rather than being eliminated.

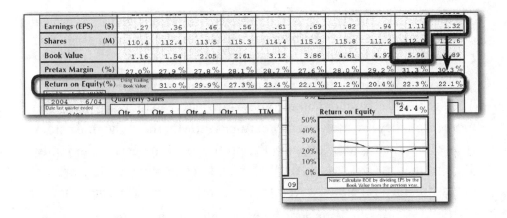

Earnings (EPS) ($)		.27	.36	.46	.56	.61	.69	.82	.94	1.11	1.32
Shares (M)		110.4	112.4	113.5	115.3	114.4	115.2	115.8	111.2	112.0	112.6
Book Value		1.16	1.54	2.05	2.61	3.12	3.86	4.61	4.97	5.96	.89
Pretax Margin (%)		27.0%	27.9%	27.8%	28.1%	28.7%	27.6%	28.0%	29.2%	31.3%	30.3%
Return on Equity (%)	Using Trailing Book Value	31.0%	29.9%	27.3%	23.4%	22.1%	21.2%	20.4%	22.3%	22.1%

Figure 13.5. Return on Equity (ROE) Using Previous Year's Equity

If you calculated ROE using the previous year's equity, as shown in Figure 13.5, then the relationship between the earnings and the equity that contributed to producing them is much clearer—a straightforward indication of the growth in the company's value and your share of it.

In general, profit margins are the most important item on the management report card. ROE (when calculated as I recommend) will generally not trend down unless profit margins, sales, or earnings growth does—in which case you're going to be looking for another company anyway.

Assessing Value

I would also make some additional observations and suggestions concerning the steps you have learned to take to analyze the price you're being asked to pay for a stock.

Estimating Future Growth

I've given you some suggestions for conservatively forecasting growth; however, there are as many different thoughts about how conservative such estimates should be as there are people who estimate. Still, no matter how experienced I get, I'm perfectly content to stick with the rules of thumb I've given you already.

What about the analysts' estimates that you can find in the *Value Line Survey*, on the Internet, in financial newsletters, or in the newspaper? Can they give you some idea of what the future holds?

Professional analysts are playing a serious game among themselves. Their reputations—and their incomes—are based on their accuracy. The more often they precisely predict earnings growth, the higher *their* stock rises within their peer group and the professional financial community. They're judged about as critically for underestimating as they are for overestimating. So either way, if they're off the mark, they can suffer.

Believe it or not, your goal is not to be accurate. Your goal is to be right. You're rewarded when your prediction is accurate, but your rewards are even greater when you prove to have underestimated. Because you have *your* money riding on your prediction, you will need to be right at least 80 percent of the time, and the best way to ensure that you'll be right is to be conservative—not unreasonably conservative, but conservative nonetheless.

As a rule, I estimate growth based upon relevant history, tempered by a reasonable decrease to elevate my confidence that I will be right. If after I have made my best estimate I find that the analysts' mean estimates are the same as mine or lower, I knock off a percentage point or two just to make sure that I'm being cautious enough to have a better chance of being right.

Companies aren't allowed to publish their own forecasts, so analysts are the ones who create earnings expectations. The surprises come when the analysts are wrong. David Dreman, author of *Contrarian Investment Strategies: The Next Generation* (Simon and Schuster, 1998), offers some statistics taken from a study of all companies followed by a minimum of four analysts—about 1,000 companies—over a 23-year period. Dreman suggests that analysts' estimates of earnings four quarters out were off by at least 5 percent 124 out of 125 times. And when the analysts were estimating five years out, the odds against their being right were 30 billion to one! Obviously some professionals are right more often than others. My point is that you have as good a chance of being right as the professionals do. The more you nestle your estimate down into your comfort zone, the more likely you are to be inaccurate on the low side—which is a fine place to be.

Estimating Future PEs

Without doubt, the most frustrating aspect of your stock studies will be trying to keep your PE forecasts within reason. This will likely be the constraint that condemns more stock candidates than any other.

I've given you a method for forecasting future PEs conservatively enough so that you will be right most of the time. By "averaging the lowest half or majority" of low values for your high and low PEs and sticking with a cap of 30 (see Chapter 10), you should rarely if ever overestimate what the future holds. But you're probably going to feel all too often that you may have underestimated.

Many investors simply use the average of the historical high and low PEs for the future value. I think that's a good idea only if you make a conscious decision to use that average after thinking carefully about it and believing that the historical high and low PEs are reasonable. This method is not conservative enough for me—especially in these times.

The PEG ratio. Many people deliberately estimate below the average just to be on the safe side. And some people use the *PEG ratio*.

The PEG ratio is calculated by dividing the PE by the estimated growth rate. For example, a company that is selling at a PE of 15 times earnings and whose earnings are expected to grow at 15 percent will have a PEG ratio of 1 to 1.

What is the value of the PEG ratio? Probably its most common use is in screening. Some experienced investors will not even look at a company that's valued at a PEG ratio of more than 1.5 or, at the most, 2 to 1.

Some investors use the PEG ratio to test the historical PE to see if it's reasonable to use it as an estimate of the future PE. Others use a PEG ratio of perhaps 1.5 to 1 as a cutoff when determining whether to invest in a company. If the estimated future earnings growth is 15 percent, the highest acceptable PE would be 22.5 (1.5 times the projected growth).

Such an approach would support my recommendation that you never forecast a future high PE over 30—which is what you'd get if you stick with 20 percent as a maximum for your forecast of earnings growth.

For my money, I'll stick with the method for forecasting future PEs that I outlined in Chapter 10!

Uncertainty bands. *Uncertainty bands* can help you assess just how erratic a company's growth can be and still be acceptable. In a word, if a company's zigging and zagging don't cut too wide a swath, you might be able to justify an expectation of sound growth.

Jay Berry, an NAIC member since 1960 and a conscientious contributor to the NAIC I-Club list (see Chapter 6), came up with the notion of uncertainty bands. He suggests that you either visualize or actually draw lines on either side of your historical trend line that encompass all or most of the plotted points on either side of that line.

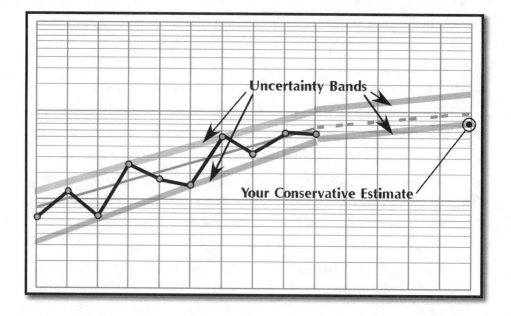

Figure 13.6. Uncertainty Bands

Then when you draw your projection out five years into the future, visualize or draw lines at the same distance from each side of that projection. Jay suggests that you assume the future value could be as far on either side of the projected value as those uncertainty bands imply. (See Figure 13.6.)

I recommend that you plot your forecast earnings where the lower band crosses the fifth year as in Figure 13.6. If you use that value as the FV (future value) to calculate the growth rate on your calculator and it's sufficient to give you your desired growth, then you can feel reasonably comfortable with your projection.

All in all, however, if the sales line is not reasonably smooth, I'd be inclined to look for another company anyway, because the kinds of things that can cause sales growth to be erratic are just the kinds of things that are likely to make the company an undesirable investment.

Evaluating Risk

The process of estimating the high price is fairly cut-and-dried, but there are some options for estimating the low price you might want to think about.

Being extra cautious. Some investors wish to be extra conservative. They factor into their forecast low price all possibilities for losing money on the investment: a declining market, an industry slump, or the worst that they think could happen if the company is the inevitable one out of five that's a loser. These cautious investors arbitrarily reduce their estimate of the forecast low price to make sure that it falls below the current price. This way the risk index remains positive, reflecting their view that there is always some risk. That's okay to do if it gives you a greater sense of security. I prefer to estimate it the same each time and let the chips fall where they may. That way, the risk index will warn me to challenge my result if it's too low.

Using the yield-supported low price. For a company that pays substantial dividends, you can use the alternative *yield-supported low price* to raise your estimate of the low price. (See Figure 13.7.)

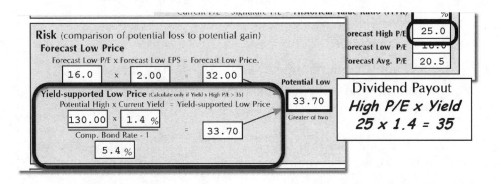

Figure 13.7. Yield-Supported Low Price

Yield is the return on a stock that its dividend represents. It is calculated by dividing the annual dividend by the price of the stock. Obviously, the lower the stock's price, the higher the yield.

It's possible for the price of a stock to decline far enough that the investment becomes attractive to investors looking for income. If, for example, the stock of a large, well-established company falls to a price so low that the yield is very near the interest on a government bond, many investors would prefer to buy the stock than to buy a bond. Not only would they receive an income that would be competitive with that of the bond, but their investment would have the potential for some good appreciation when the stock's price resumed its growth. This low price could be construed to be a *resistance point* (to borrow a term from the technical analysts) because income investors would likely jump in and prevent the price from going lower.

This alternative method of arriving at a low price is useful only for companies whose dividend payout is substantial. The projected dividend payout is the product of the current yield and the forecast high PE. If it comes to 35 or more, it might be worth the trouble to calculate the yield-supported low price.

To do so, first look in your newspaper under "U.S. Securities" for the securities whose maturity date corresponds to your forecast date. Find the approximate yield for those securities.

Then calculate the yield-supported low price as follows:

Potential high price × Current yield ÷ (Competitive bond yield −1)

Here's an example:

Assume that the competitive bond yield is 6.4, the current yield is 1.4 percent, and the potential high price is 130.0

Yield-supported low price = 130 × 1.4 ÷ 5.4 = 33.70

If this value is higher than your forecast low price, you may substitute it for the forecast low instead.

Because you'll rarely be interested in large companies that pay high dividends, you'll seldom use this option, but it can give such companies a little help when you assess their rewards and risks.

These are but some samples of the lore and wisdom that you'll gather as you progress on your investment journey. Some of the ideas are good, and some of them simply aren't for you—just as it will be with other new things you'll hear along your way. Take them all with a grain of salt and test them with your common sense. That common sense is your most important asset on your road to becoming a successful investor. And as I said at the outset, the things that appear to be over your head are likely things you don't need to know!

Remember, too, that *experience is a license to lower your standards*! You'll usually do better by keeping your standards high!

Conclusion

W
ell, that's it from my point of view. You now know more than the average stockbroker about investing and about how businesses run. You should be able to deal with them with confidence. (If you doubt this, just ask them questions about what you've learned and see how they respond. You might be surprised.) I hope that you've enjoyed reading this as much I've enjoyed writing it. Your pleasure will have only begun here and should extend to your future investment experience.

I've given you all I think you need to know to be a successful investor. The rest is simply a matter of getting in there and doing it—and not being intimidated by the things you don't need to know. Other things that you may find to be important to you will be important because your own curiosity draws you to them. And that can be fun, too.

I wish you a happy and prosperous journey as you Take Stock and build your successful financial future.

The Stuff You Don't Need to Know

At the end of Chapter 4, I touched on the things you don't need to know and why you don't need to know them. Notwithstanding the fact that knowledge of these tools of management's trade is not required for you to be successful, you might want to learn about them just to indulge your curiosity. In this appendix, I have exposed you to just a few of the more common ratios and metrics used in the process of running companies and referred to by those professionals who try to second-guess their managements.

Financial vulnerability deals with the management of debt, leverage, and capitalization. *Operational vulnerability* deals with such things as production control, inventory and collections.

Financial Vulnerability
Liquidity

These ratios relate to how easy it is for a company to come up with cash if it's needed.

➤ **Current Ratio** (Current assets ÷ Current Liabilities). There is no real benchmark; but, if it's too low, then the company might not be able to meet its current obligations; if too high, it might not be making the best use of its assets. However, each case is different, and "low" or "high" most often depends entirely upon company policy, industry practice, and deliberate decisions by management.

➤ **Quick Ratio or "Acid Test"** (Current Assets less Inventory ÷ Current Liabilities). This is a more "accurate" basis for evaluating the company's ability to pay off its current liabilities, because inventory is not as liquid (can't be used to raise cash as easily) as the other current assets. The same observations apply.

Leverage

Using OPM (other people's money) to make money is smart business as long as the company doesn't go over its head in debt. From the perspective of a shareholder, the more revenue-producing assets a company can put into play without requiring more money from the shareholders, the better. The downside, of course, is the vulnerability issue and what creditors might do if the income dries up enough to make servicing the debt difficult or impossible.

Common ratios to evaluate leverage are:

➤ **Debt to Assets** (Total Debt ÷ Total Assets). This ratio measures the proportion of that the company owes to the value of all of the company's assets, in effect telling you what portion of the company's possessions have been acquired with other people's money. This usually includes short-term obligations and intangible assets and is a rather broad measure as is its rule-of-thumb: a figure below 50 percent is considered okay; above, more risky. Here, as with most ratios, you don't simply go from good to bad by sliding over the line from 49 to 51 percent. Just how "risky" is a matter of a whole lot of other interdependent considerations and criteria as well.

➤ **Assets to Equity** (Total Assets ÷ Shareholder Equity). This is another means of measuring what proportion of assets are attributable to debt. Anything beyond 100 percent is encumbered. This is the third component of ROE (return on equity), which we discussed elsewhere.

➤ **Debt to Equity** (Total debt ÷ Shareholder Equity). This is another view of the relationship between total debt and the value of the shareholders ownership. Total debt may or may not include obligations due within five years. Some say that 100 percent debt/equity is the "limit of prudence," which, roughly translated, means that any time the company owes more than it's worth, it's not a good thing.

➤ **Debt to Capital** (Long-term Debt ÷ Total Capitalization). This ratio is perhaps the most "refined" measure of leverage that indicates what portion of the company's funding was borrowed. From a lender's point of view, this is an important measure, and many lending agreements contain restrictions that are based upon this figure. However, in recent years, growing emphasis seems to be placed upon the ability of the company to service its debt rather than on the static relationship recorded in the balance sheet. Benchmarks for this ratio vary all over the place, depending upon the industry; and, there are exceptions for every example, which makes it virtually impossible for any but an insider or a professional familiar with the company and its industry to draw any sensible conclusions from it. The figure of 33 percent for manufacturing companies is frequently thrown around. Philip Morris (MO), putting aside the ethical considerations, was always considered an excellent investment, although most of the time leveraged to the point where more than 60 percent of its capitalization was debt. Go figure!

I would not base an investment decision on any of the ratios just discussed. Their most useful purpose could be to call your attention to possible upcoming changes in your quality criteria and might lead you to be more vigilant about them as you manage your portfolio.

Debt Service

➤ **Interest Coverage** (EBIT ÷ Interest ["EBIT" means "net profit (Earnings) Before Interest and Taxes])" This is a new term for you that, except for this definition, you don't really have to know about. What this tells you is how many times over the company could pay the interest on its indebtedness from its earnings.

Obviously, the company only needs to pay it once, but, needless to say, the higher the number, the better. The more "slush" the company has between what it earns and what it must pay out to service debt, the less vulnerable it will be in hard times.

237

What's a good number? Where is the "comfort level"? Again, it depends on a lot of different things. But, common sense would tell us that a company with a large supply of cash or a healthy "quick ratio"—another number that, to be "healthy," also depends on a lot of other things—would be less vulnerable than another having the same interest coverage but without those advantages.

➤ **Interest and Principal Coverage** [EBIT ÷ (Interest + Adjusted Principal Repayments)]. This similarly indicates not only the company's ability to handle interest, but to handle the payments on the principal as well. ("Adjusted Principal Repayments" takes into account the pretax value of the principal, because those payments are not tax-deductible, whereas the interest is.)

Operational Vulnerability

Most tools involve either items from the income statement or items that match information from the income statement with those on the balance sheet.

Income Statement Ratios

➤ **Income/Expense Analysis** (Income/Expense for specific line item ÷ Net sales). It's important for management to monitor what percent of sales was contributed by each of the different product lines, for example, or to analyze and compare from week to week—or for whatever period the data is collected—what percentage of net sales was used to pay for raw materials or labor or transportation. These are supposed to stay within certain reasonable values, and any significant change alerts management to find out the cause and do something about it.

➤ **Profit Margins** (Profits ÷ Net Sales). Of those income statement items, the bottom line is the bottom line. The most important by far is the relationship of profit to revenue—or profit margins. Though there is value in comparing all levels of profit to revenues (for example, gross profit, pretax profit, net profit), we prefer to look at pre-tax profit because it is the clearest measure of how management handles the expenses over which they have control. We have included this as one

238

of the crucial criteria in judging management's ability to sustain a company's growth and is therefore among those ratios you *do* need to know about.

Income Statement/Balance Sheet Ratios

Other ratios involve specific balance sheet items. And these are usually compared with either sales or profits. When they are compared with sales, the ratios are often expressed as "turnover"; when they are compared with shareholder equity, they are referred to as "return."

➤ **Asset turnover** (Revenues ÷ Assets). This is an indication of how much revenue is generated by every dollar of assets.

➤ **Inventory turnover** (Revenues ÷ Inventory). This approximates how many times a year the inventory is sold. It is a metric by which management can tell whether it's maintaining a reasonable amount of inventory for its sales activity. Higher values are usually better because it means that management is being efficient enough not to have to worry about being left with stuff it can't sell. Of course, if it's too high a number, it might run out of stuff and upset its customers. If it's too low, it's not pushing enough out the door. These values depend on whether average, beginning, or ending inventories are used and how the company costs out its inventory. (This can also be expressed as the number of days inventory lasts by calculating it the same as Accounts Receivable (see the following ratio).)

➤ **Accounts Receivable turnover** (Accounts Receivable ÷ Revenues ÷ 365). This approximates how many days it takes to collect the average receivable. When this figure is compared with credit terms (such as "net 30"), it is a measure of how effective credit policy is and how well collections are going.

➤ **Accounts Payable turnover** (Accounts Receivable ÷ Revenues ÷ 365). This has the same implications with regard to the company's ability to pay its bills. Comparing the result with the aging statement (which shows how much debt is current, is within 30, 60, 90, or more than 90 days old) can tell you how well the company is doing in that regard. It's doubtful that you could get your hands on the aging statements, however.

➤ **Return on Assets** (Profit ÷ Assets). This ratio tells you how much profit is made from every dollar's worth of assets.

➤ **Return on Equity** (Profit ÷ Shareholder Equity). Return on equity (ROE) can be broken down into the product of three components: net profit margin (net profit ÷ revenue) × asset turnover (revenue ÷ total assets) × balance sheet leverage (total assets ÷ shareholder equity). (See Chapter 13 for a more complete discussion of ROE.)

The balance sheet indicates a *condition*. This condition is of interest to those that are naturally concerned with the gloomy side—vulnerability *if* things go wrong. Your interests definitely lie on the brighter side—what you would expect to happen when things go right—at least 80 percent of the time! Both you and the managements of your companies need to be more interested in those companies as going concerns. So your focus needs to be on the income statement that deals with *performance*, and the only effective measurements that you need have been covered adequately in earlier chapters.

Resources for the Computer User

Here I'd like to recommend resources that will best serve your needs as you pursue your new investing skills using a computer. I'll talk about these tools in the order in which you will use them:

1. Data/Prospecting.

2. Stock analysis.

3. Portfolio management.

4. Portfolio tracking/record-keeping.

ICLUBcentral, a Cambridge, Massachusetts company, is now the sole provider of all of the stock analysis software products I recommend herein—products that have been tried and proven by a substantial number of users. They also provide the accounting software that is recommended by NAIC used by most of its investment clubs.

Data/Prospecting

➤ **Stock Investor PRO** (American Association of Individual Investors (AAII; *www.aaii.com*). A superb screening tool that provides a database containing more information than you could possibly use for more than 9,000 publicly traded stocks. Ships on a CD each month that contains not only the software but data in a format that is suitable for import into the analytical products described here.

Stock Investor PRO's interface is well thought out and easy for a novice to master. And adequate help is available. The program provides a full complement of preset screens that deliver some excellent prospects for study. These include the Inve$tWare Quality screen, which I contributed to the product, the parameters of which match the criteria for quality I have described in this book. Users can use any of 1,500 variables to create their own screen or modify existing ones. Stick with the PRO version; the lower-cost version does not include the data nor does it provide as many options for screening as the PRO version.

➤ **NAIC Prospector** (ICLUBcentral; *www.iclub.com*). The official NAIC software for screening company data files. Requires a subscription to NAIC's Online Premium Service (OPS). The software allows you to search NAIC's electronic datafiles to find companies that fit the profile for which you're looking. Also contains preset screens with stated objectives, or users can define their own screens. The interface is not difficult to work with, and it has become a mature and high quality program over the years.

➤ **OPS Data** (National Association of Investors Corporation (NAIC); *www.better-investing.org*). Arguably one of the most valuable benefits of NAIC membership, OPS data is, alone, worth the cost of membership if you have the software that can make use of it. Where people originally would have to enter data in the software products manually, they can now import all of the required data to perform a stock study with a simple mouse-click. Delivered online, the data is updated daily.

Stock Analysis

Technamental investing has been practiced in one fashion or another for five decades, but it boasts only a few software products that deliver all or most of what the technamental practitioner needs. Until recently, the only products available for this purpose were those developed for NAIC or marketed to its membership.

242

The compact disk included with this book will allow you to get a jump-start on your analysis. It is based on the Technamental Stock Study Worksheet described in these pages, and it will allow you to enter the necessary data and see the results. Check out the information inside the back cover for a full description. In addition, demo copies of each product listed here may be found on the CD and installed so you can try them out for yourself.

➤ Take $tock (ICLUBcentral; *www.iclub.com*). The simplest and most intuitive tool for the technamental analysis of common stocks. In the basic mode, you simply enter the symbol or name for the company you wish to analyze. The program will do the rest. Downloading more than 100 items of fundamental information about the company from the Internet, it will do all of the analysis described in this book, including making all of the decisions, conservative forecasts and estimates, and will deliver a simple report that assesses the quality of the company on a scale of one to 10. If the company is of investment quality, it will also provide the highest price at which the return and risk criteria would be met. You may print out the Technamental Stock Study Worksheet (TSSW) or a simple summary telling you reasons for buying it and items to be cautious about.

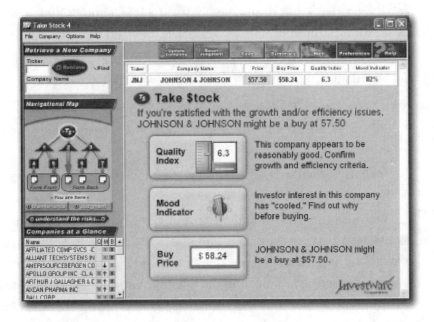

Figure B.1. Take $tock produces instant result

Users can learn all about the concepts with convenient access through a "Concepts" button to an in-depth description of the methodology and the concepts behind it.

Operating in advanced mode, users can override the automated judgments and enter their own. Stock studies may be saved in a database, and tools are available to quickly analyze which of them may suffer when new data is available.

Although Take $tock makes use of the same data source as OPS data, a separate OPS subscription is not required. A Take $tock subscription, which include the continuing use of data, technical support, and free updates to the program, is renewed annually for a modest price.

➤ **NAIC's Take $tock** (NAIC; *www.better-investing.org*). This version of Take $tock was developed at the request of NAIC and differs from the original version in only two ways. The first is a "wizard" teaching tool that presents users with five screens showing the company's growth characteristics and PE history. Users answer a question after viewing each screen to progress to the next one. When they are complete, the program then delivers the reports as described for the original version.

The second distinction is that, instead of the TSSW, the NAIC version prepares and prints the NAIC Stock Selection Guide (SSG) in addition to the summary of reasons to buy and items to check.

As with the original version, users may operate the program in advanced mode and may also disable the wizard if desired.

➤ **NAIC's Investor's Toolkit Version 5** (NAIC; *www.better-investing.org*). NAIC's official stock analysis product and NAIC's best-selling product for more than a decade.

Includes all of the NAIC forms for stock analysis, comparison, and portfolio management.

Provides the user with all opportunities to apply educated judgments, forecasts, or estimates, and offers a "Judgment Audit" to review those judgments for reasonableness. The depth of instruction, the context-sensitive help, and the documentation that accompanies the program have earned the Toolkit its place as the favorite of NAIC investors.

The strong point of the Investor's Toolkit is its user interface, which is easy for the newcomer and equally comfortable for the power user. The Toolkit does everything that NAIC recommends for the stock selection process and follows NAIC protocols to the tee.

The Investor's Toolkit also has very powerful tools for coordinating your Internet activities: conducting research, pricing stocks, buying and selling using your online broker, updating data, and accessing your club's Website.

The latest version of the Toolkit has added intuitive but sophisticated tools for implementing both your defensive and offensive portfolio management tasks.

➤ **NAIC Stock Analyst** (ICLUBcentral; *www.iclub.com*). Another program that has matured with time. Although its interface may be a little less intuitive than that of the Toolkit, it adds features that appeal to the more experienced or advanced user and approaches some of the protocols for applying judgment in a slightly different manner.

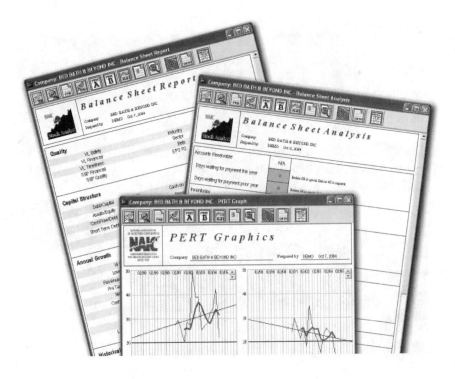

Figure B.2. NAIC Stock Analyst adds extra features and graphs

Replete with additional graphs and opportunities to graph additional data, and with functions that examine the balance sheet and some of the other metrics I have placed in the "you don't *need* to know" category, those who wish to explore those interesting things have the opportunity to do so with this program.

It, too, has all of the functions and forms prescribed by NAIC for acquisition, comparison, and portfolio management.

Portfolio Management

Both the Investor's Toolkit and Stock Analyst Plus contain all of the tools NAIC provides for portfolio management. These tools correspond to the printed forms NAIC provides to help users monitor the fundamentals of the stocks in a portfolio and apply both the defensive and offensive strategies described in Chapter 12.

However, Investors Toolkit 5 has taken the process to a new level by offering a concise process by which those strategies may be easily and effectively implemented.

Figure B.3. The Investor's Toolkit facilitates portfolio management strategies

The program will remind you when new data is due to be reported for each company you are following, in as many portfolios as you may wish to work with. You may then update that data and, should any company's fundamental performance fall below your expectations, it will present that company for you to evaluate and make a decision as to whether to hold it or sell it.

It will also notify you when the price of any stock causes the return and/or risk to fall below your threshold and give you the opportunity to evaluate whether to keep it or not.

An Overview screen (see Figure B.3) shows you the pertinent detail about each company in your portfolio and shows you the dollar-weighted, aggregate performance statistics for your portfolio as a whole. You can make hypothetical changes in your portfolio and see the effect of those changes should you decide to execute them.

Portfolio Tracking/Record-Keeping

Portfolio tracking is satisfying because it tells you just how well you're doing, and Uncle Sam (who wants to know how well you're doing, too) requires it.

Both Intuit's *Quicken* and Microsoft's *MS Money* are very popular and effective tools for tracking your progress, which is the fun part after you've done all of the tasks required to manage your portfolio. One of these programs is all you need if your activity is reasonably stable and infrequent and if you don't have a lot of reinvestment activity.

➤ **Portfolio Record Keeper** (Quant IX; *www.quantixsoftware.com*). If you wish to do a more detailed job of record-keeping—or need to because you are reinvesting dividends and must provide detailed records to the IRS—you may wish to use Quant IX's Portfolio Record Keeper, an excellent program crafted especially for individual investors who want to watch closely the performance of their portfolios. It accomplishes all that you need for reporting to Uncle Sam, and that's not the half of it.

Almost any information you could want about the performance and makeup of your portfolio you can either find in an existing report or create a report that can tell you, and you can see your results graphically. The most recent version is state of the art, and even a novice can learn to get the most out of it practically over night.

With the software covered here, you should have all you need to take advantage of your computer to perform your investment chores easily, accurately, quickly, and painlessly—and even have a little fun while you do it. Everything you need to do to be a successful investor you can do with a computer in just a few hours a year!

Using the CD-ROM

The CD-ROM that comes with this book is intended to be a fun companion to the text that will help you get the most out of it. Simply insert the CD into your drive and, within 10 or 15 seconds, it should launch on its own. From there, it is self-explanatory. (If it doesn't launch, select the CD-ROM drive in "My Computer" on your desktop, right-click on the icon, and then select "Auto Play" from the displayed menu.)

Once you have installed the software, you'll find it is divided into three significant parts:

1. A refresher quiz for each chapter.

2. A section to assist you in finding the necessary information on financial statements or the Value Line Survey page.

3. A stock analysis section.

Take the test. Consisting of anywhere from five to a dozen questions for each chapter, you may select this option and quiz yourself about what you've read. This will reinforce the concepts and help you see what you might have missed. It's an interactive lesson that will tell you the right answer and explain it.

I suggest that you take the short quiz after finishing each chapter.

Deal with data. This section will be of greatest value to you after you have studied Chapter 4, which discusses and defines in simple terms what data you will need to use for your stock analysis. The software will ask you to find the essential data wherever you can. The two most readily available sources are financial statements, which companies are generally pleased to provide, and the *Value Line Survey*, which you can obtain in most libraries. The software will let you know when you have produced the wrong or right answer and help you to locate the data if you don't know where to look.

Analyze a company. Starting with Chapter 7, you will take all the steps necessary to analyze a stock, using ABC Company, a fictional company whose data are very real. You may import the data for ABC Company—or enter the data yourself from a copy of a *Value Line Survey*—and follow along with the text.

When you have completed the study of ABC Company, you may then import the data for any of 30-odd other companies from whose data you can learn to apply the things you've learned. (These companies are included to show you good and bad investment candidates and not to suggest the purchase of these stocks. The data provided may be out of date and prices out of any reasonable range.) This will give you enough practical experience to be ready to do stock studies yourself. Experiment with different prices to see the effect on the result; for example, try the buy price for each.

You can also use this software to analyze stocks of your own choosing for which you have obtained the necessary data.

Software demos. On this disk, you will also find demo copies of four software products: two versions of Take $tock, NAIC's Investor's Toolkit, and NAIC's Stock Analyst.

My suggestion is that you first take a look at the "Original Version" of Take $tock. This most closely follows the illustrations in this book because the worksheet that is at the core of that software was used in preparing the illustrations within. (You can learn more about this product and even download the instruction manual by pointing your browser to *www.iclub.com/products/itakestock.asp*.)

The other products are used primarily by NAIC members who have been made familiar with the Stock Selection Guide—NAIC's form for implementing the principles as taught by them.

If you like the demos and wish to purchase the software, you can do so by following the directions offered when you launch the demos.

I suggest you hold off installing any demo until you have become thoroughly familiar with the stock analysis software contained in the third segment of the CD-ROM. That way you'll be able to understand and get the most out of the demo software before the 30-day demo restriction expires.

I hope you will enjoy using the software created for you and will see just how easy it is to make educated decisions about investing in common stocks on your own. It is also my wish that you will use the software to enrich both your learning and your bank account.

Index

About the Author

Ellis Traub lost virtually everything but his good job as an airline captain when in his early 40s. Scared out of the stock market until he retired in his late 50s, he would have repeated the experience with his pension had he not discovered the National Association of Investors Corporation (NAIC), whose principles he learned and embraced, subsequently taught, and still shares with standing-room-only audiences across the country.

He subsequently turned his financial life around, developed the computer software used by most NAIC members to implement those principles, and, in this book, shares with you the principles of "technamental investing" based on what he learned and applied successfully.

He recently sold the software company he founded and lives with his wife, Dianne, in South Florida, continuing to accept invitations to speak when he feels he has an opportunity to help people avoid the pitfalls he encountered along the way.